SAMSON

SECRETS TO DESTROYING YOUR LIFE AND MINISTRY

J. Christopher McMichael

Published by Engrafted Word Church
5 W. Broad Street, Cookeville, TN 38501
www.EngraftedWord.org

ISBN: 978-0-9823390-6-0

Unless otherwise indicated, all Scripture quotations are from the King James Version of the Bible.

Scripture quotations labeled NASB are from the New American Standard Bible® (NASB), Copyright © 1960, 1962, 1963, 1968, 1971, 1972, 1973, 1975, 1977, 1995 by The Lockman Foundation. Used by permission.

Scripture quotations marked NIV are taken from the Holy Bible, New International Version®, NIV®. Copyright © 1973, 1978, 1984, 2011 by Biblica, Inc.™ Used by permission of Zondervan. All rights reserved worldwide. www.zondervan.com. The "NIV" and "New International Version" are trademarks registered in the United States Patent and Trademark Office by Biblica, Inc.™

Scripture quotations marked NLT are taken from the Holy Bible, New Living Translation, Copyright © 1996, 2004, 2015 by Tyndale House Foundation. Used by permission of Tyndale House Publishers, Inc., Carol Stream, Illinois 60188. All rights reserved.

Cover layout by Darrell Kerley
Maps by Manda McMichael
Cover Painting: *Samson* 1887, Solomon J. Solomon. On display at the Walker Art Gallery, Liverpool.
Back Engraving: *Samson Carrying Away the Gates of Gaza* 1866, Gustave Dore. Sixty-fourth of 241 engravings done for the 1843 French translation of the Vulgate Bible, published as La Grande Bible de Tours in 1866.

Printed in the United States of America

Dedication

This book is dedicated to the late Kenneth James Vaughn, my first real pastor and father in the faith. He pioneered a church and a move of God. It is upon his shoulders I now stand and upon the foundation of his work I now build. He believed in me when others didn't.

Table of Contents

PART 1
Historical Setting and Theological Overview

PART 2
The Four Destructive Secrets of Samson's Life

Foreword
By Dr. Mark T. Barclay

I have read Chris McMichael's first book and all of his articles. I have enjoyed them all and rejoiced in the fact that one of my sons in the faith is such a great writer. However, this is by far my favorite and perhaps the best thing he has ever written. Job well done, Chris!

Samson has always been one of the saddest accounts in the Bible, yet possibly my favorite. There is so much to learn from it, and so much of it reflects people's lives today. In all my studies on this topic, I have not read after anyone who exposes the hidden truths and dangers as Chris does in this book. I enjoy the straight-to-the-point style Chris has—no fluff, no apologies, no sugar coating. This is not a placebo, like many books being written today. This is the real medicine.

Wow… though I loved every chapter, I especially clung to chapter five on being alone. I pastor many people and hundreds of ministers. I have witnessed many times the application of what Chris is referring to in this chapter. I have spoken globally to so many ministers and believers about not allowing the devil or people to isolate them. The enemy always strikes the straggler and the ones falling behind or wandering around on their own. No matter who they are or how long it takes, they almost always end up in shipwreck. What a shame.

It is always sad to hear of so many Christians self-destructing, knowing it was self-afflicted. It was avoidable. Their story should have been different. This is one of the reasons I love this book so much. It points out to everyone how to avoid such self-afflictions and stupid mistakes. If you read and obey the warnings in this book, you will avoid shipwreck. You will build a great testimony in Christ. You will be a victor!

I hope that every Christian everywhere gets a copy and studies it—may we not just read it, but actually take time to study and meditate and look deep into our lives and examine ourselves to eliminate all sin and worldly, human practices that will eventually snare us and even damn our souls.

When you are finished reading and studying the content of this book, make yourself a list of the secrets on a small card and keep it in your wallet. Look at it often and take a deep examination of your life. It could save you a lot of pain and even conceivably save your life.

-Dr. Mark T. Barclay

Introduction

The life of Samson was both magnificent and disappointing. Poised to become the greatest of Israel's judges, he succumbed to the basest of indulgences. Although his leadership should have ignited a great revival for all of Israel, he instead became a mere reflection of his nation's own spiritual condition. Like Israel, he had the promised potential of a consecrated leader, yet he managed to live as an unfaithful, harlot-chasing ruffian.

There are so many lessons to be learned from the famous herculean judge. Reared by two of the most dedicated parents in the entire Bible narrative, Samson was blessed of God from his youth and anointed to begin to eradicate Israel's famous enemy—the Philistines. Sadly, his leadership went nowhere and he ultimately committed suicide as a slave.

Instead of eliciting national pride, Samson became one of Israel's greatest disappointments. As *Keil and Delitzsch* perfectly summarize, "it looks as if Samson had dishonored and fooled away the gift entrusted him, by making it subservient to his sensual lusts, and thus had prepared the way for his own ruin, without bringing any essential help to his people."[1] Where did Samson go wrong? Where did he veer off track? What can today's ministers and Christians learn from this tragically short-circuited ministry?

Though he is remembered as a failure, we must be fair and acknowledge that only four chapters (96 verses) have been dedicated to his life and ministry. It is easy to be critical of Samson, but what would our story look like if our life's highlight reel only covered our failures? We cannot forget that Hebrews 11 ultimately commemorates him as a

---

[1] C.F. Keil and F. Delitzsch, "The Book of Judges," in *Commentary on the Old Testament*, Vol. 2 (Hendrickson Publishers, Inc., 1989), 400.

man of faith, no doubt because he faithfully executed the will of God in the early stages of his judgeship.

I personally believe Samson's self-destructive arc is specifically recorded as a warning to us today. It is a template of "what not to do." In studying the divinely recorded story of this famous judge, a pattern arises; a pattern that, unfortunately, many unknowingly continue to follow today. Let us consider the life of Samson lest we follow in his tragic footsteps, dying blind, bound, alone, and surrounded by the enemies of our God.

My personal study of Samson began many years ago when a minister I greatly respected died prematurely. His unexpected passing left many believers confused, hurt, and shaken. Here was a man who had spent over 30 years living for the Gospel, preaching far and wide, winning the lost, writing books, teaching others how to succeed in ministry, and who was even mightily used in the Gifts of the Spirit with numerous notable miracles credited to his ministry (and the power of Jesus Christ, no doubt!). Yet he died early. He failed to finish his race. Many reasoned, "If he can't finish his race, who can?"

As time passed, his premature death bothered me more and more. I wanted to know what happened. His early death contradicted Psalm 91:16, "With long life will I satisfy him . . ." This great preacher didn't get to see this promise. He still had plans to do even more for the Lord, and so I know for a fact he wasn't satisfied yet.

I began to ask the Lord what went wrong. I also began to look into his private life (I was in a place that afforded me this unique opportunity). After about two years of prayer, Bible study, and questions, the Lord began to teach me about Samson, and more specifically what I have come to call the *Curse of Samson*. I discovered that the dead preacher in question, one of my greatest heroes in the faith, had actually begun to slowly sear his conscience, defiling his life and ministry with private sin.

Some years prior to his death, he had begun to tolerate little improprieties here and there. These slowly opened the door to greater sins he would have passionately condemned years earlier. The confusing aspect of this perversion was that he actually remained mightily used of God until he died. Though his public life appeared clean, his private life grew dirtier and dirtier, just like Samson's. And like Samson, his destruction came suddenly and without remedy (Proverbs 6:15; 29:1).

I have since seen this pattern—this *Curse of Samson*—play out over and over again. I have even come to recognize it in the news reports and biographies of contemporary ministry failures. The pattern is simple: first, a humble, clean servant of God begins to be used of God. Second, as the humble servant's ministry grows, his or her relationship with God is slowly and subtly neglected, thus opening the door for sin and compromise. Next, as sin and compromise grow, the servant's ministry continues to grow, often helping even more people than in their early, clean days. God then offers opportunities to repent, but they are rejected. From the pulpit, the servant even preaches the answer to his or her own problem, even giving their own call to repentance, but to no avail. Finally, the servant becomes nearly bigger than life until the secret sins of the perverse private life explode, either destroying the servant or their ministry (sometimes both). The catastrophic ministry implosion always leaves God's people reeling, the Lord's name maligned, the servant's family ashamed, and God's enemies emboldened.

This book has been written in two parts. Part One evaluates the historical setting and provides a brief theological overview of a few Old Testament precepts. Though it might be tedious reading for some, I have endeavored to simplify this rich but complex season in Israel's history. It would be very useful to read Judges 13-16 before continuing with this book (or even the entire book of Judges for that matter). Part Two is a principalization and application of the dangerous patterns of Samson's lifestyle. It contains an exposition of four destructive practices I have observed in the life of Samson.

The primary purpose of this book is to warn believers concerning these behaviors. As a pastor and missionary, I see Christians everywhere unknowingly repeating the same practices in their own lives, almost always to their own detriment. Though this book was written primarily with the Gospel minister in mind, this by no means would exempt the rest of the Body of Christ from the truths contained herein.

This isn't just a warning for the minister. It's a warning for every believer. If any man thinks he stands, let him take heed lest he fall. It is my prayer and hope that this book would help many Christians run their race to the finish line and hear our Lord say, "Well done, thou good and faithful servant. Enter thou into the joy of the Lord."

Christopher McMichael

PART I

Historical Setting
and
Theological Overview

.

Chapter 1

A Brief History of Israel:
From Abraham Through the Time of
the Judges

In 1874 B.C.[2], God appeared to Abram and made His covenant with him (Genesis 12:1). The Abrahamic covenant was inherited by Isaac, the son of promise, who then begat twin sons, Esau and Jacob. Esau, being the firstborn, was entitled to the family inheritance, but in a moment of petty carnality, he sold his birthright to his younger brother for a bowl of soup. Jacob famously wrestled with the angel of the Lord, and as a reward, his name was changed to *Israel*, which means "wrestles with God" (which Israel certainly has done ever since). Jacob, now renamed Israel, begat 12 sons and one daughter by his two wives and two concubines. These sons ultimately became the 12 tribes of Israel.

About 1676 B.C., due to the jealousy of some of his older brothers, Joseph, the second youngest son of Jacob, was beaten and sold into slavery for about 13 years, eventually ending up in Egypt. By the divine hand of God, Joseph arose to the position of prime minister (viceroy) in order to guide Egypt through a seven-year savings program in preparation for seven years of prophesied famine.

In 1654 B.C., the severe famine brought Joseph's long separated family down into Egypt from Canaan in the north in search of food and provisions. This reunited Joseph with his family and caused Israel, now many hundreds in numbers, to dwell in Egypt. Joseph instructed his

---

[2] All dates are according to Mattis Kantor, *The Jewish Time Line Encyclopedia* (Aronson, 1992) and crosschecked by Robert P. Killian.

brethren to request the land of Goshen and to let the Egyptians know that Israel was a shepherding people (for the Egyptians detested shepherds).

As the nation of Israel grew in numbers, the pharaohs succeeding Joseph feared the swelling population of Israelites and so moved to enslave them. Their abuse continued until 1444 B.C. when Moses delivered them from Egypt (430 years from when God made his covenant with Abraham in Haran, but after only 210 years in Egypt). By now they were no longer a tribe of several hundred, but a nation estimated to be closer to two million in number.

After the Exodus from Egypt, Israel failed to trust God's provision, tempting Him 10 times[3], and was therefore relegated to wandering in the wilderness for 40 years until every faithless Israelite died off. After 40 years, the children of Israel were then led into the Promised Land by Joshua, Moses' protégé, servant, and military general. This began a new season in Israel's history. For the next 28 years, Joshua led Israel in battle after battle until 31 kings succumbed to his military prowess.

After Joshua died, Israel was ruled by elders for 17 years until the last elder who had seen the great works of the Lord by the hands of Joshua had died. Then a new generation arose. This was a generation that did not know the mighty works of God (Judges 2:7); this began an era defined by barbaric lawlessness referred to as *The Time of the Judges*. This time period lasted for 351 years and was marked by 15 judges. This era lasted until Israel requested its first king in 1010 B.C. Samson lived and judged Israel near the end of the Time of the Judges, having died in the year 1061 B.C.

To reframe the above history in terms of generations, consider the following timeline: Israel was in Egypt for 210 years, or four generations (Gen. 15:16), the better part of which they were enslaved and oppressed. Israel then spent 40 years, or approximately one generation, under Moses' leadership in the wilderness. After Moses died, Joshua led Israel

---

[3] The 10 temptations of God by Israel (Numbers 14:22): Exodus 14:11; 15:24; 16:2; 16:27; 17:2; 32:1; Numbers 11:1; 11:4; 12:1; 14:2.

into the Promised Land and numerous military campaigns for 28 years. Joshua's leadership and the preceding elder leadership lasted for 45 years, or approximately one generation. This means Israel went from being slaves to nomads to conquering settlers in just three generations— the generation that came out of slavery, the generation that was raised in the wilderness, and the generation that walked into the Promised Land. If this pattern were applied to your family, it would mean your grandparents were slaves, your parents were nomads, and now you are the conquering settler of God's Promised Land. God moves quickly with those who want to move with Him!

The Time of the Judges

The Time of the Judges began in 1359 B.C., following the death of the last elder who knew Joshua and saw the mighty works of God. It may help the Bible student to understand up front that the book of Judges chronicles the early and often barbaric days of Israel establishing itself as an infant nation. This season was defined by Israel still settling Canaan and battling the wicked inhabitants that stood in their way.

This period of Israel's history also presents us with the sense of a national identity struggle for the Israelites as they battled to maintain their dependence on Jehovah even while all the tribes spread out into their new territories. This struggle is best understood when we consider that for 40 years all of Israel had lived together in one giant nomadic camp with their entire existence revolving around the Tabernacle of Moses and the glory of God. This nomadic camp enjoyed the fire of God by night, the glory cloud by day, and the supernatural provision of manna and quail, with only the occasional military skirmish. The unity of vision and purpose afforded by these close living conditions were quickly lost as the tribes of Israel dispersed across their inherited land (see Map 1).

In possessing the Promised Land, Israel went from being a nomadic people dwelling in tents, still thinking like Egyptian slaves, to an agricultural people living free on their own farms and in their own

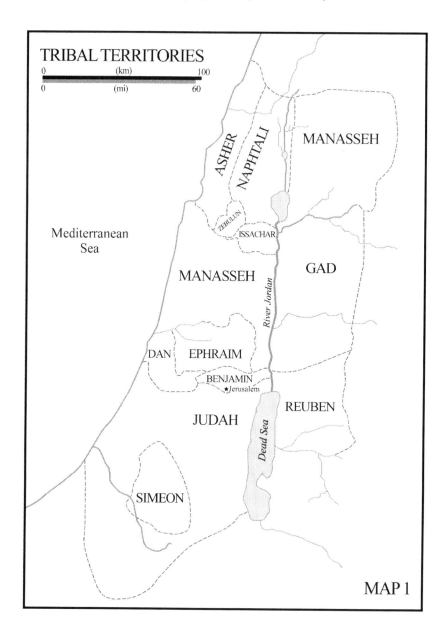

towns—no longer subsisting on divine provision but on whatever they could grow or raise, having never been an agrarian people. As if this wasn't difficult enough, Israel had to make these existential transitions while fighting against pagan neighbors who wanted to either oppress them, kill them, or entice them into intermarriage and idol worship.

Lawlessness: The Spirit of the Age

The author of Judges (probably Samuel) reminds us several times that the Time of the Judges was a period when Israel had no king and "every man did that which was right in his own eyes" (Judges 17:6; 18:1; 19:1; 21:25). This phrase perfectly summarizes the spirit of lawlessness. Lawlessness is every man doing what seems right to him.

Proverbs casts judgment upon those who practice lawlessness saying, "There is a way that seemeth right unto a man, but the end thereof are the ways of death" (Proverbs 14:12; 16:25). As is always the case, it was the practice of lawlessness that brought God's people much suffering and judgment when all God wanted to do was bless them.

Lawlessness *isn't* the total rejection of civil, biblical, or spiritual laws. It is the mixing of those laws with carnal whims, convenient approaches, and degenerate reasonings, creating something entirely new while altogether rejecting any law that is found to be unfavorable.

Lawlessness is deceptive. It is the picking and choosing of the laws you do and don't want to obey. It can sound "churchy" and Christian, but it is still totally rejected by God Almighty. Lawlessness is dangerous because it mixes in enough of the Word of God with our own selfish ambitions and sinful tendencies, fabricating some new kind of corrupt doctrine to follow. Those deceived by lawlessness believe they are still right with God simply because they have applied Bible terms to their compromised endeavors.

The New Testament warns us about the spirit of lawlessness. Jesus said that in the last days lawlessness would abound, producing a cold, calloused love (Matt. 24:12).[4] Paul also prophesied about lawlessness in the last days:

---

[4] From the Greek *psycho:* to grow cold

For the secret power of lawlessness is already at work; but the one who now holds it back (restrains it) will continue to do so till he is taken out of the way.
2 Thessalonians 2:7 NIV

There is a "secret power" to lawlessness. Part of that power is its ability to deceive people into their own destruction. How? Lawlessness rejects whatever law is standing in the way of sinful pleasure. Lawlessness is tempting because it grants access to sin and its short-term pleasures. It is the subtle embracing of what you want over what God wants for you. Lawlessness is people doing what they want, when they want, as they want. That may sound like freedom, but nothing could be further from the truth.

Lawlessness is the primary fruit of the antichrist spirit, and it is rebellion against God. Paul revealed in the previous verse that lawlessness requires restraint. The laws of our life, be they civil laws, biblical laws, or traffic laws, provide restraint against rebellion and danger while keeping society safe, orderly, and peaceful. When someone yields to the antichrist spirit they will begin to cast off restraint and do what seems right in their own eyes. This will always result in danger, disorder, and pain in their life.

Lawlessness is the natural tendency of mankind and the sin nature. Without a voice of oversight or accountability, carnal man will always track towards the self-destruction of lawlessness. This is why God has always had a leader over His people and why Israel descended into lawlessness once Joshua and the elders died. Even when God did raise up judges to lead them, the people refused to listen (Judges 2:16-17). The result was the same as it has always been—oppression, chaos, defeat, fear, and hurt.

The last five chapters of Judges are often referred to as appendices due to the post-script manner of their inclusion to the rest of the book. These five chapters document two stories that succinctly demonstrate the "spirit of the age," the spirit of lawlessness—each man doing what was right in his own eyes. According to Mattis Kantor, these two incidents took place during the judgeship of Othniel the first judge.[5] These two stories are representative of the two major sins of Israel during this time: idolatry and sexual perversion. These two examples demonstrate how Israel practiced lawlessness. They didn't totally abandon all the Laws of Moses, just those laws that inconvenienced them. We will look a little deeper at these stories in the next two sections. Pay special attention to how both stories of lawlessness involve a Levite—someone who should have been both a keeper and practitioner of the Law.

The Cult of Micah (Judges 17 & 18)

The first story explains the development of the Cult of Micah (Heb. *Pessel Michah*). Micah (not to be mistaken with the prophet Micah who lived some 600 years later) was an Israelite who made a graven idol with his mother's money. Along with the molten image, Micah built a house of gods, filled it with wooden idols, and consecrated one of his sons to be the priest over his cult. When a wandering Levite passed through his town, Micah recognized the man's higher pedigree (he was, after all, a Levite) and he quickly recruited him to be the new priest over his cult. According to Judges 18:30[6], this Levite-for-hire was none other than Moses' grandson Jonathan. Jonathan gladly accepted the offer to play priest for a paycheck and became one of the Bible's first hirelings. He

---

[5] Mattis Kantor, *The Jewish Time Line Encyclopedia*, 40.

[6] The King James Version uses the name Manasseh due to a hanging 'n' over the name *Moseh* in some original texts. All modern translations and commentators agree that the original name is Moses. "The Talmudists declare (B. B. 109b) that the "nun" was inserted in the name of this Moses out of respect to the great lawgiver, and that the former's name was changed to "Manasseh" because the wickedness of Jonathan resembled that of King Manasseh. They identify Jonathan with the above-mentioned Shebuel (*ib.* 110a), saying that he was so named because he repented (שב אל = "he returned to God"). The same interpretation is given by the Targum to I Chron. xxiii. 16." Hirsch, E. G., Seligsohn, M., Schechter S., "Jonathan, Jehonathan," *Jewish Encyclopedia*. New York: Funk & Wagnalls Company. 1906. Vol. 7, P.232.

and his sons "were priests unto the tribe of Dan until the day of the captivity of the land," that is, until the Philistines stole the Ark of the Covenant.

How could there be such perversion and idolatry in Israel? Because there was no righteous leadership in this season, and every man did that which seemed right in his own eyes. By mixing some of the Mosaic Law with personal preferences, the Cult of Micah embodied the practice of lawlessness. He wanted something to worship, but Jehovah was too inconvenient so he created idols. He used silver that his mother had dedicated to the Lord to sculpt the idols he placed in a consecrated house. After building a house of worship and installing idols, he created an ephod just like what a real priest was commanded to use. He appointed one of his sons to be the first priest, but deep down he was unsettled because he knew that the Law only allowed for Levites to be priests. Imagine his delight when he was able to hire a wandering Levite.

Once he had his hireling Levite, the cult of Micah was complete. Though his new "church" was a total sham, Micah was deceived by his own lawlessness enough to say, "Now know I that the LORD will do me good, seeing I have a Levite to my priest" (Judges 17:13). What Micah failed to see was that he had, in effect, pioneered a new gospel. He created a system of worship that mixed the holy with the profane. Unfortunately, God doesn't bless the holy half and overlook the profane half. He overlooks the holy half and curses the whole thing because of the profane half. What deception to think that serving God on your own terms will bring His blessing upon you!

Bizarrely enough, men from the tribe of Dan saw that this man Micah had a cult of idols *and* a priest to oversee the worship thereof, and they decided to steal them both. These Danites took the idol and the priest and set them up in the northernmost city of Laish, changing the name from Laish to Dan. Thus the famous city of Dan was inaugurated with idol worship and a false priesthood. This cult of convenient worship and idolatry, created by one man's lawlessness, continued for 297 years, led by the apostate offspring of Moses until Eli the high priest, the second-to-last judge, died and the ark was stolen from Shiloh (1 Sam. 4).

The Benjamite War over a Brutalized Concubine

In chapters 19-21 of Judges, the author records a second story to exemplify Israel's lawlessness in the arena of sexual perversion. This story deals with the brutal gang rape of a Levite's concubine by a group of Benjamites. Here the barbarism and anarchy of the time are horrifically demonstrated when the traveling Levite, not feeling safe in a strange town (Jebus), opted to take evening refuge in the nearby town of Gibeah inhabited by his brethren the Benjamites. Remember, at this time Israel is co-inhabited by Israelites and Canaanites. Not trusting the Jebusites, the Levite assumed he would be safe among his fellow Israelites, the Benjamites.

To his horror, and with recalls of Lot's experience in Sodom, the men of Gibeah wanted the Levite for their perverse pleasure. The Levite gave his concubine to the mob who then proceeded to gang rape her all night long until she died. In disgust and desirous of justice, the Levite cut the corpse of his concubine into 12 pieces and delivered them to the 12 tribes of Israel as a testimony against the tribe of Benjamin.

The "lewdness and folly" of Benjamin so disgusted the rest of Israel that the remaining tribes declared war against their own brethren. When it was all said and done, over 90,000 Israelites died settling a perverse and prideful issue that initially cost one woman her life. As further punishment against Benjamin, the rest of the tribes forbade any of their daughters to marry a Benjamite. However, to prevent the total extinction of Benjamin, the Benjamites were permitted to kidnap a virgin from Shiloh during the annual feast to the Lord in Shiloh.

Needless to say, the entire story is bizarre and barbaric, and that is exactly the point. Why all the violence, brutality, barbarism, kidnapping, and war? This is the ultimate end of lawlessness. These were brutal times when there was no king, and "each man (and tribe) did that which was right in his own eyes."

The Pattern of Lawlessness and Judgment

Israel's lawlessness during the time under the judges followed a simple four-step path to judgment and oppression. Step one involved choosing to neglect the primary commandment to drive out the inhabitants of the land. By allowing the enemies of God to remain their neighbors, Israel easily set themselves up for steps two and three. Step two: since these pagan people were now Israel's neighbor, Israelites eventually fell in love and married them (Judges 3:5-7). Intermarriage to the enemy caused the third step to come naturally: they began to worship their spouses' pagan gods. Step three forced God's hand to bring about the fourth step: judgment through an oppressor, i.e., the neighbor they neglected to drive out or destroy. This process reveals a spiritual principle modern Christians should heed: the enemy you don't destroy will eventually destroy you. The pattern repeated during the Time of the Judges is perfectly summarized in Judges 2:11-19 (NKJV):

> **Then the children of Israel did evil in the sight of the LORD, and served the Baals; and they forsook the LORD God of their fathers, who had brought them out of the land of Egypt; and they followed other gods from among the gods of the people who were all around them, and they bowed down to them; and they provoked the LORD to anger. They forsook the LORD and served Baal and Ashtoreths. And the anger of the LORD was hot against Israel. So He delivered them into the hands of plunderers who despoiled them; and He sold them into the hands of their enemies all around, so that they could no longer stand before their enemies. Wherever they went out, the hand of the LORD was against them for calamity,**

as the LORD had said, and as the LORD had sworn to them. And they were greatly distressed. Nevertheless, the LORD raised up judges who delivered them out of the hand of those who plundered them. Yet they would not listen to their judges, but they played the harlot with other gods, and bowed down to them. They turned quickly from the way in which their fathers walked, in obeying the commandments of the LORD; they did not do so. And when the LORD raised up judges for them, the LORD was with the judge and delivered them out of the hand of the enemies all the days of the judge; for the LORD was moved to pity by their groaning because of those who oppressed them and harassed them. And it came to pass, when the judge was dead, that they reverted and behaved more corruptly than their fathers, by following other gods, to serve them and bow down to them. They did not cease from their own doings nor from their stubborn way.

Israel's stubbornness made them weak before their enemies. *The Song of Deborah and Barak* succinctly described Israel's cycle of lawlessness and judgment as follows, "They chose new gods; then was war in the gates" (Judges 5:8a). Israel's worship of false gods gave their enemies supernatural permission to oppress them.

Meet the Opposition

The book of Judges opens with a very sad account of Israel's lazy disobedience and its subsequent ramifications. In the first chapter of Judges, we read that numerous tribes (Manasseh, Ephraim, Zebulun, Asher, Naphtali, and Dan) all failed to defeat the wicked inhabitants of their territory as they were commanded to do. Only Judah, Simeon, and the house of Joseph attacked enemy cities. These enemies included the

Ammonites, the Philistines, the Amorites, the Hittites, the Jebusites, the Perizzites, the Hivites, the Mesopotamians, the Moabites, the Canaanites, the Sidonians, and the Midianites.

These various nations were territorial. No single enemy nation or kingdom inhabited the entire Promised Land, but rather they each dwelt in regions: e.g., the Philistines dwelt in the southwest region, the Moabites had their kingdom in the southeast, the Ammonites inhabited the land east of the Jordan, the northern inhabitants are often collectively referred to as Canaanites, etc. (see Map 2). In other words, what would eventually become the single nation of Israel was, at this time in history, a land divided among several pagan kingdoms.

It is helpful to understand the history, origins, and territories of some of the famous enemies of Israel. Their details are recorded in the Bible for a reason, and understanding some of these facts only enriches our study of Judges and ultimately Samson. It is also interesting to note how many of these enemies were the direct descendants of Noah, Abraham, and Lot.

The six major enemies in the book of Judges are:

Canaanites/Amorites—The Canaanites were the descendants of Canaan, the son of Ham, Noah's cursed son (Gen. 10:16). Amorite and Canaanite are somewhat interchangeable terms, with Canaanite being a very general term usually ascribed to the inhabitants of the lowland and coastal territories. The Amorites were a smaller group among the Canaanites dwelling in the northern area of the Promised Land. Sihon and Og were two famous Amorite kings killed by Moses (Num. 21:21-35). Barak's military campaign led 10,000 soldiers from Naphtali and Zebulun against the Canaanites in the north at the River Kishon in the valley of Megiddo (Judges 4:6-7).

Amalekites—The Amalekites traced their lineage through Esau's grandson Amalek (Gen. 36:12). This meant the Amalekites were Abraham's descendants (see Map 2). Amalek was the chief of the

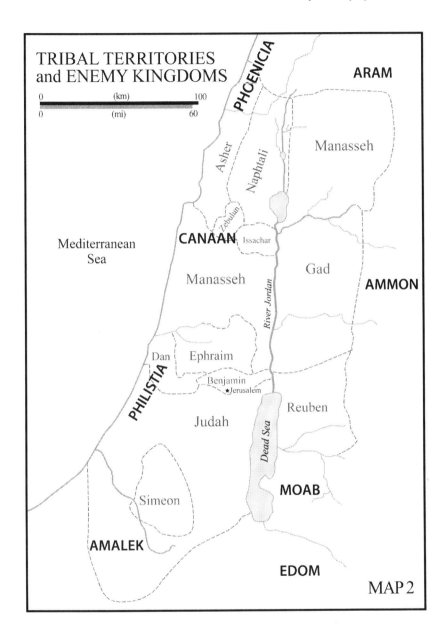

Edomites (Esau's lineage, Gen. 36:16), who then became the Amalekites. They inhabited the southern desert region of Israel, west of the Dead Sea all the way down to the Gulf of Aqaba. Gideon fought against the Amalekites and the Midianites (Judges 6:3; 7:12).

Ammonites—The Ammonites descended from Benammi, the incestuous son from Lot's drunken affair with his younger daughter (Gen. 19:32-38). The Ammonites dwelt east of the Jordan. During the Time of the Judges, the Ammonites made war against the Israelites (those from the tribe of Gad) over a land dispute. The land in question originally belonged to the Amorites, but God gave it to Israel when the Amorites (Sihon) fought against Moses and the children of Israel (Numbers 21:21-25). The Amorites previously took the same territory from the Moabites. Israel possessed this territory for 300 years before the Ammonites decided they wanted it (Judges 11:26). Jephthah fought against the Ammonites and subdued them.

Midianites—After Sarah passed away, Abraham remarried a woman named Keturah and had six more sons (Gen. 25:1-2). One of these sons was named Midian, and he became the father of the Midianites. They dwelt mainly to the southeast of the Dead Sea. Gideon was responsible for inflicting much hardship upon the Midianites.

It is believed that the Midianites were a confederacy of tribes more than a single kingdom possessing a territory. One of the tribes contained within the Midianite confederacy was the Ishmaelites. These were the descendants of Ishmael, Abraham's son by Hagar. It was the Midianites, specifically Ishmaelites, who purchased Joseph from his brethren then sold him to Potiphar (Gen. 37:25-28). The Midianites that Gideon destroyed were also Ishmaelites (Judges 8:24).

Moabites—The Moabites descended from Moab, Lot's son born of his incestuous encounter with his older daughter after their escape from Sodom (Gen. 19:32-37). The Moabites dwelt on the eastern side of the Dead Sea. Balak was the famous Moabite king who hired the soothsayer Balaam to curse Israel while they were still in the wilderness (Numbers 22:4-6). Eglon was the obese king of the Moabites during the Time of the Judges. The Israelite judge Ehud assassinated Eglon with a left-handed dagger. Ruth was also a Moabitess. Jewish tradition holds that Ruth was either the daughter or granddaughter of King Eglon, who was a descendant of Balak.

Philistines—The Philistines descended from a man named Casluhim, the son of Mizraim (meaning *Egypt* or *Land of the Copts*). Mizraim was the father and progenitor of the Egyptians (Gen. 10:13). Apparently Casluhim moved away from his father and located directly adjacent to Egypt's northeastern border. The Philistines have the longest recorded Bible history of interaction with Israel, beginning with Abraham's dealings with Abimelech, king of the Philistines (Gen. 20:2; 26:1), running on and off again until the days of King Hezekiah, a span of over 1,000 years.

Abraham and Isaac had peaceful dealings with the Philistines in their lifetimes and even made covenants with them. During the Exodus, God did not lead Israel out of Egypt through Philistine territory in order to avoid war between the two peoples and the crushing blow a violent encounter would have had on Israel's morale (Ex. 13:17). God reminded Joshua that Israel had yet to tackle the Philistine's territories and that a great work remained (Joshua 13:1-3). Therefore, various battles with them ensued thereafter. Shamgar and Samson are the only leaders in the book of Judges charged with afflicting them. They are referenced as having been led by five lords, each over a different major city: Gaza, Ashdod, Ashkelon, Gath, and Ekron.

After Samson's death, first Eli then Samuel continued battling and rebuffing the Philistines until there was a temporary peace during the life of Samuel. King David ultimately put down the Philistines in a victory that lasted until the days of King Jehoram, nearly 150 years later. King Uzziah, King Ahaz, and King Hezekiah also fought successful campaigns against the Philistines. However, they were never completely wiped out. As a side note, the Greek word for Philistine is *Palestina*, hence Palestine and Palestinian.

Chapter 2
Old Testament Judges

The Old Testament term *judge* can be difficult to relate to for today's Westerner. Our modern understanding of a judge usually envisions a man or woman in a black robe with a gavel in hand. The judges (Heb. *shoftim*) in the Bible are described as "deliverers," "saviors," or "defenders" (Judges 3:9,15; 6:36; 8:22; 10:1,12; 13:5; 18:28) because they saved, delivered, and defended Israel from the hands of their oppressors.

Translated as "judge" or "ruling leader," the term as used in the book of Judges never describes a singular national leader over a united Israel as was Moses, Joshua, and the kings; instead, it is used to describe a tribal leader. The book of Judges does not record a single judge as having jurisdiction over all of Israel, but rather only over a tribe or two, four at most.[7]

The enemies and oppressors in Judges were territorial and therefore, generally only afflicted the tribes that had settled in their domain (see Map 2). Remember, when Israel possessed the Promised Land, numerous kingdoms still inhabited it. Joshua did not drive out all of the inhabitants during his 28-year tenure as national leader and military general. The preexisting kingdoms possessed the land, but Israel was to dispossess the land. The battle for dispossession would take place in numerous territories, led by 14 judges[8], over a span of 351 years.

Each tribe had its own enemy to battle. For example, Othniel only made war with the Mesopotamians. Shamgar only contended with

---

[7] Gideon led men from four tribes: Manasseh, Asher, Zebulun, and Naphtali (Judges 6:34-35).

[8] This number excludes Abimelech, the pseudo-judge.

Philistines. Gideon only fought with the Midianites and Amalekites. God raised up these tribal leaders to deliver Israel from whatever enemy was oppressing their respective region and people. In this regard, the burden of taking the Promised Land was distributed among the tribes of Israel (see Map 3). Each tribe had to do their fair share. Only the tribes of Reuben, Asher, Gad, and Simeon lack a representative judge in the Bible.

It is important to note that the judges didn't just wage war; they were also civil leaders to their tribes and resolved intratribal conflicts. A judge's responsibilities in this era included peacemaking, law giving, deciding-of-matters, and dispute settling. Deborah, the only female judge, established her headquarters in Mount Ephraim under a palm tree known as "the palm tree of Deborah" (Judges 4:5). It is here Deborah "held court." All of Israel came to submit to her judgment and counsel. At her judgment, disputes were settled after opposing cases were presented. Following in the spirit and example of Moses, the judges were also responsible for making Israel to "know the statutes of God, and his laws" (Exodus 18:16).

Israel's Fifteen Judges

There are 13 judges in the book of Judges, but 15 judges total. Theologians divide the 13 *shoftim* in the book of Judges into seven minor judges and five major judges, with Abimelech the sixth judge often categorized as a pseudo-judge due to his ignominy. The first judge the Lord raised up was Othniel, followed by Ehud, then Shamgar, Deborah and Barak, Gideon, Abimelech (the pseudo-judge), Tola, Jair, Jephthah, Ibzan, Elon, Abdon, and finally Samson.

The book of Judges only covers the lives of the first 13 judges. Eli and Samuel are considered the final two judges of this time period, but their lives are recorded in 1 Samuel. Jewish tradition holds that Samson died a year after Eli became the high priest, producing a unique and brief overlap of two judges. This was also the same year the prophet Samuel was born. God used all three of these Bible heroes—Samson, Eli, and Samuel—to fight against the Philistines.

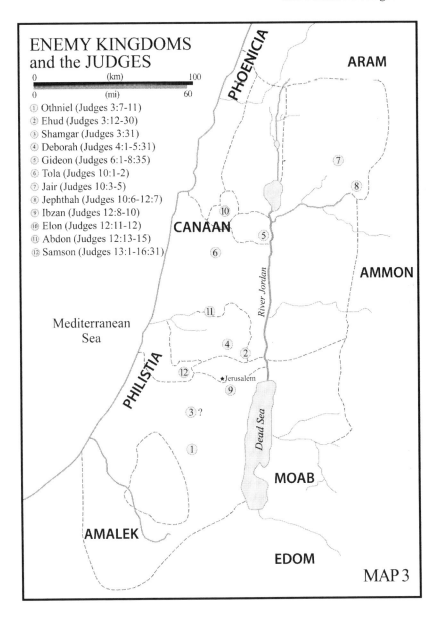

ENEMY KINGDOMS
and the JUDGES

0   (km)   100
0   (mi)   60

① Othniel (Judges 3:7-11)
② Ehud (Judges 3:12-30)
③ Shamgar (Judges 3:31)
④ Deborah (Judges 4:1-5:31)
⑤ Gideon (Judges 6:1-8:35)
⑥ Tola (Judges 10:1-2)
⑦ Jair (Judges 10:3-5)
⑧ Jephthah (Judges 10:6-12:7)
⑨ Ibzan (Judges 12:8-10)
⑩ Elon (Judges 12:11-12)
⑪ Abdon (Judges 12:13-15)
⑫ Samson (Judges 13:1-16:31)

PHOENICIA

ARAM

CANAAN

River Jordan

AMMON

Mediterranean
Sea

PHILISTIA

★Jerusalem

Dead Sea

MOAB

AMALEK

EDOM

MAP 3

The Seven Minor Judges

The seven minor judges mentioned in the book of Judges are considered minor, or lesser, because there is far less detail given concerning their lives and ministries. These are Othniel, Shamgar, Tola, Jair, Ibzan, Elon, and Abdon. Consider how little is said about Othniel the first judge:

> **And when the children of Israel cried unto the LORD, the LORD raised up a deliverer to the children of Israel, who delivered them, even Othniel the son of Kenaz, Caleb's younger brother. And the Spirit of the LORD came upon him, and he judged Israel and went out to war: and the LORD delivered Chushanrishathaim king of Mesopotamia into his hand; and his hand prevailed against Chushanrishathaim. And the land had rest forty years. And Othniel the son of Kenaz died.**
>
> **Judges 3:9-11**

Only three verses are dedicated to the first judge and kid brother to Caleb. Now consider the one verse given concerning Shamgar, the third judge: "And after him was Shamgar the son of Anath, which slew of the Philistines six hundred men with an ox goad: and he also delivered Israel" (Judges 3:31).

The Pseudo-Judge

We must briefly discuss the pseudo-judge, Abimelech, though the Scriptures never refer to him as a judge, nor do they ever describe his three-year reign as "judging Israel." Abimelech was the son of Gideon by his Canaanite concubine from Shechem. The entire ninth chapter of Judges is dedicated to Abimelech, but his Canaanite pedigree, wickedness, and underhandedness exempt him from any place of honor (or worthiness of the term "major judge"). After the death of his father Gideon, Abimelech killed 69 of his 70 half-brothers, with only Jotham escaping. Abimelech succeeded in gathering the Shechemites, his mother's people, unto himself and they made him king in Shechem. His reign lasted three years before a woman killed him when she threw a large stone from a tower, striking him in the head. Ultimately, his leadership only affected small regional clans. Theologians have called his reign a usurpation of power.

The Seven Minor Judges Continued

After Abimelech, God raised up Tola the seventh judge. Tola's tenure is summarized in two verses:

> **And after Abimelech there arose to defend Israel Tola, the son of Puah, the son of Dodo, a man of Issachar; and he dwelt in Shamir in mount Ephraim. And he judged Israel twenty and three years, and died, and was buried in Shamir.**   **Judges 10:1**

Tola is followed by Jair, who is chronicled in only three verses. He judged Israel for 22 years and is remembered for having 30 sons who rode upon 30 donkeys and oversaw 30 cities, collectively called *Havothjair*, or "the villages of Jair." This possibly indicates that Jair's domain was only 30 cities.

The 10th judge was Ibzan whose ministry is also chronicled in only three verses. He was known for having 30 sons and 30 daughters and taking in 30 daughter-in-laws. He only judged Israel for seven years.

Ibzan was succeeded by Elon, a Zebulonite who judged Israel for 10 years. Nothing at all is said about Elon except for where he was buried. The final minor judge, Abdon, the 12th named in Judges, had 40 sons and 30 nephews who were known for riding around on 70 young donkeys. Abdon judged Israel for eight years.

As previously stated, there just aren't many details given about the minor judges. With the exception of Othniel, Shamgar, Tola (and the pseudo-judge Abimelech), it does not appear that the minor judges engaged in any sort of military skirmishes with their surrounding oppressors. It may be that their leadership only involved judging between matters of intratribal controversy, as Moses did before his correction by

Jethro and subsequent institution of the wilderness judges in Exodus 18:13-26. Regardless, the Bible records no dereliction of duty or sin from the minor judges. It appears these men were successful and faithful in their duties. This is significant because, though lacking the extraordinary power and anointing of the more famous Samson, they were still successful in fulfilling their assignment. This fact only further indicts Samson for his ministry failure.

The Five Major Judges

There are five major judges discussed in the book of Judges. These are Ehud, Deborah/Barak, Gideon, Jephthah, and Samson. They are considered *major* for the same reason the books of Isaiah, Jeremiah, Ezekiel, and Daniel are called Major Prophets—more detail is given concerning their lives and ministries. Incidentally, Gideon, Barak, Samson, and Jephthah are also mentioned in Hebrews 11 as great men of faith. Only Ehud and Deborah are excluded. From their stories we can clearly see examples of how the judges were usually regional or tribal in their leadership, and not national. We can also further see how the Israelite oppressors were likewise territorial and not nationwide.

Ehud the Benjamite (Judges 3:12-30)

Ehud, a Benjamite whose tribe had settled along the Jordan River at Jericho, delivered Israel from the obese king Eglon, a Moabite. Eglon gathered the Ammonites and the Amalekites to fight with him against Israel at Jericho, taking the eastern city. This only affected the Israelites dwelling in that area, namely the tribes of Benjamin and Ephraim. After Ehud slyly assassinated King Eglon, he gathered the men of Benjamin and Ephraim together and led them in a military victory against the Moabites. Their military endeavor reclaimed territory along the Jordan, killed about 10,000 Moabites, and subdued Moab. Under Ehud's leadership, Israel had peace and rest for 80 years.

Deborah and Barak the Naphtalite
(Judges 4:1-5:31)

Deborah was a centrally located prophetess who judged Israel from the hill country of Ephraim, about five miles north of Jerusalem. Her leadership appears only to have involved rendering judgments for the Israelites when they had disputes among themselves (Ex. 18:13,16).

Though Joshua had previously destroyed the Canaanite capital city of Hazor, King Jabin had rebuilt the city located in the northern territory possessed by Naphtali. This made the Canaanites and King Jabin Naphtali's responsibility. When we are introduced to Barak, we find that God had already commanded him to arise and lead 10,000 men from Naphtali and Zebulun (two neighboring tribes afflicted by Jabin and the Canaanites) against Sisera, the Canaanite general. When the prophetess Deborah sent for the reluctant military general Barak (over 100 miles north of her home), he was hiding out in the refuge city Kedesh of Napthali trying to escape the call of God. Jewish tradition holds that Barak and Deborah were husband and wife, he being also known by the name Lapidoth (Judges 4:4).

Gideon the Manassahite (Judges 6:1-8:35)

Gideon was of the tribe of Manasseh. He led four tribes in victories against the Midianites (descendants of Abraham by his wife Keturah; Gen. 25:1-2) and the Amalekites (descendants of Esau's grandson, Amalek). God gathered to Gideon 32,000 men from the clan of Abiezer (a clan within Manasseh) and from the tribes of Manasseh, Asher, Zebulun, and Naphtali. Mindful that a large army could easily assume credit for a military rout, God permitted the fearful to return home, and 22,000 left. The ranks were further reduced at the water when 300 men who drank water from their hands were conscripted into Gideon's army. With this small group of 300 men, Gideon fought against the armies of the Midianites and Amalekites.

Jephthah the Gileadite (Judges 11:1-12:7)

Described as a man of valor, Jephthah was the son of Gilead (of the tribe of Manasseh) and a harlot. His home territory placed him in Ammon's domain. Being a half-breed, his brethren ran him out of town until they needed his military cunning to help them overcome the onslaught of the Ammonites. He returned from exile in Tob to be the leader of his father's people and defeat the Ammonites. He did not rule over all of Israel, just a portion of the tribe of Manasseh, and the Gileadites. His battles with the Ammonites stayed east of the Jordan River. Jephthah is best known for the rash vow he made to God in exchange for military victory (Judges 11:30-40).

Samson the Danite (Judges 13:1-16:31)

This brings us to the fifth major judge (but 13th out of 15 total judges) and the subject of this book: Samson, of the tribe of Dan—a tribe whose territorial inheritance placed them deep in the heart of Philistine country. Alas, Samson's calling was to beat back the Philistines. He was "to begin to deliver Israel from the Philistines." Without question, he had the most unique anointing of all the judges and certainly the greatest miracles. He judged Israel for 20 years but never afforded them any peace or leadership. The work he began would be continued by Eli the high priest and then concluded in that season by the prophet Samuel (1 Sam. 7:13-15). The secret to his divine power and strength rested in the consecration of his Nazirite vow.

Chapter 3

The Nazirite Vow
(Numbers 6:1-21)

The key to Samson's strength rested in his consecration to Jehovah God. Like so many famous Bible heroes, Samson's special purpose for God was evident at birth (e.g., Isaac, Moses, Samuel). However, what made Samson different was the angelic commandment for him to live as a Nazirite[9] his entire life. The term *Nazirite* means, "consecrated or devoted one." The Nazirite vow was a unique vow for the Old Testament believer and is mentioned in Numbers 6, Judges 13-16, Lamentations 4:7, and Amos 2:11. Along with Samson, Samuel and John the Baptist were also lifelong Nazirites[10] (see 1 Sam. 1:11; Luke 1:15). It is therefore critical that the reader have a working understanding of the Nazirite vow in order to fully appreciate the recklessness and carelessness that led to the downfall of Samson.

A Lifestyle of Consecration

The term Nazirite comes from the Hebrew word *nazir* meaning, "to dedicate, consecrate, separate, to devote oneself, or to keep sacredly separate." The emphasis and heart behind the Nazirite vow is that of total dedication, consecration, and devotion to God. The individuals who chose to invoke the Nazirite vow did so of their own free will in special devotion to Jehovah. The vow was generally intended to be for a limited

---

[9] I will use the more modern spelling of *Nazirite*, which is closer to the Hebrew and avoids any confusion with *Nazarene,* of which there is no association.

[10] It is commonly held that Paul also had a Nazirite vow in Acts 18:18.

amount of time, though some might choose to live as a Nazirite indefinitely. When invoked, this vow testified to everyone that the devotee had completely given him or herself over to God for that season.

The Nazirite vow held three requirements that originated in the Levitical priesthood. By invoking a Nazirite vow, the average Israelite could live for a season at a level of consecration similar to that of the priests; however, it must be pointed out that the Nazirite restrictions were actually much stricter than the similar demands placed upon the priests.

Being a Nazirite made the adherent holy unto the Lord, and therefore, greatly increased their opportunity to be used by the Lord. The overall purpose of the vow is summarized in Numbers 6:8, "All the days of his separation he is holy unto the LORD." This level of consecration seems to have elevated the Nazirite to a temporary spiritual status on par with the prophets (see Amos 2:11-12).

The Three Restrictions of a Nazirite

The Law of Moses prescribed three restrictions that accompanied the Nazirite vow. Certainly, any vow toward God begins in the heart, but some sort of action must accompany it. If an Israelite decided to invoke a Nazirite vow, God required the following three actions: 1) prohibition of all fruit of the vine, 2) refraining from cutting the hair for the length of the vow, and 3) avoiding contact with any dead person.

At the end of the self-determined vow, the Nazirite would then present themselves and a very costly set of offerings to the high priest. Their hair was then cut at the door of the Tabernacle of the Congregation and burned in the fire under the peace offering (also called a fellowship offering). After this, the devotee was free from his vow and could return to living as a normal Israelite. If at any point during the vow the Nazirite violated any of these tenets, their entire vow would be forfeited, requiring the devotee to start over (with a shaved head).

No Fruit of the Vine

The first restriction of the Nazirite vow was a total abstinence from all fruit of the vine. This included raisins, grapes, grape skins, grape seeds, grape juice, wine, vinegar of every kind, and every kind of intoxicating drink. Part of this requirement hearkens to the standard placed upon the priests:

> **Do not drink wine nor strong drink, thou, nor thy sons with thee, when ye go into the tabernacle of the congregation, lest ye die: it shall be a statue for ever throughout your generations: And that ye may put difference between holy and unholy, and between unclean and clean;** **Leviticus 10:9-10**

The Nazirite vow places a higher standard upon the devotee, requiring abstinence not just from wine but also from all fruit of the vine. This is obviously a stricter prohibition than that required of the priesthood. The other implication of the grape restriction may have to do with a forced inconvenience upon the life of the vow maker.

Grapes were one of the staple crops of ancient Palestine and therefore, one of the critical foodstuffs for an Israelite. To require an Israelite to abstain from anything related to the grapevine was to inflict a severe cultural inconvenience. Gone were grapes and raisins as a calorie source. Gone was any food cooked in grape seed oil. Gone were any juices, alcoholic or otherwise, made from grapes. The entire diet of a Nazirite would have been affected. The desires of the flesh would have to be kept in check at each meal. This first restriction of the Nazirite vow teaches us that consecration to God will always be inconvenient to the flesh.

No Razor Upon the Head

The second restriction of the Nazirite vow also parallels the Levitical priesthood (Lev. 21:5). The priests were commanded to keep their hair a certain way. They could not shave their heads or the corners of their beards. The Nazirite's obligation went much further than the priest's concerning the hair of his head. He was to never cut his hair during the course of his vow. The hair requirement of a Nazirite's vow visually testified to everyone the length of the Nazirite's vow. Longer hair indicated a longer time spent in this special season of consecration, while shorter hair (but longer than usual) testified of a shorter season spent thus far in consecration.

This second requirement testifies of the obvious outward manifestation a consecrated lifestyle should produce. Though we don't consecrate ourselves to God for people, if people can't see a difference in our lives, we must question how consecrated we really are. Perhaps our consecration is truly like the Nazirite's hair: the longer we stay consecrated, the more apparent it should become to everyone.

No Contact with the Dead

The Nazirite could not touch a dead person or even enter the room where a dead person was. This third and final rite of the Nazirite is also rooted in priestly requirements; howbeit the priests were permitted to deal with the dead, but only if they were immediate family. The Nazirite, on the other hand, was not permitted to defile his consecration; not even for his immediate family—once again demonstrating that the Nazirite vow was much stricter than the requirements placed upon the priests.

Even if by some happenstance someone died unexpectedly while sitting beside a Nazirite, he or she was instantly considered defiled and had to start over by shaving their head and then offering two doves or two young pigeons; one for a sin offering and one for a burnt offering. Then, with his or her freshly shaved head and on the same day as their atonement, the Nazirite had to restart their vow for the same amount of time they had originally purposed in their heart to fulfill. All prior time spent as a Nazirite was forfeited by their exposure to a dead person.

This third requisite has several applications for us in the New Testament. First, it's not how we start but how we finish our race that matters. Second, we must be mindful of dead things in life and even more cautious of those who flirt with death. Third, we cannot slow down to chase dead family. Let the dead bury the dead. And finally, we don't get to quit just because we defile ourselves midrace. We must get back up. We must rededicate and re-consecrate ourselves and keep on running!

As a critical note, there are no implications from Scripture that Samson was held to this third Nazirite obligation as a judge. It is difficult to imagine how he could have maintained this obligation as a warrior anointed to slay the Philistines "hip and thigh." It also appears that Samson was not held to the vine prohibition, as is evident by the departure of God's Spirit only after his hair was shorn. Special attention must be paid to what the angel required of Samson's Nazirite vow. A quick review of the angel's instructions to Manoah indicates that the only direct commandment given concerning Samson was that "no rasor shall come on his head: for the child shall be a Nazarite unto God from the womb" (Judges 13:5). This is confirmed by Samson when he fatally confides in Delilah, "There hath not come a rasor upon my head; for I have been a Nazarite unto God from my mother's womb: if I be shaven, then my strength will go from me, and I shall become weak, and be like any other man" (Judges 16:17).

The Votive Sacrifice

Once the vow was completed, the Nazirite had a costly set of offerings to present, which is interesting considering the devotee had just finished what was probably the holiest season of their entire life. The Nazirite was to present a year-old spotless lamb for the burnt offering, symbolizing consecration to God. In addition, they presented a spotless year-old ewe lamb for the sin offering, atoning for any committed sins. And for a peace offering,[11] they were to present a spotless ram with grain

---

[11] The peace offering symbolized a meal of fellowship between the Nazirite and God, indicating God's acceptance of their repentance and total consecration.

offerings, drink offerings, and a basket of the finest leaven-free bread coated with olive oil.

Then, assuming the LORD received the fellowship offering, which was always indicated by a supernatural fire consuming the offering (Lev. 9:24; Judges 6:21; 13:20), the Nazirite was to shave "the hair that symbolizes their dedication" and present it to the priest who would then burn it in the fire under the fellowship offering. This service was concluded by the priest giving the now former-Nazirite a shoulder of the ram and one thick loaf and one thin loaf of bread from his peace offering, symbolizing the Lord's acceptance and invitation to come and eat with Him at His table. Thus, the Nazirite vow was fulfilled and the Israelite could return to a normal life.

Chapter 4
Trained to Succeed

By all accounts, Samson should have been the most successful judge in Israel's history. He was born to holy parents of the tribe of Dan. His mother, whose name we do not know, was barren. An angel supernaturally informed her that, though she was currently barren and childless, she would conceive a son. This son was to be special on three counts: 1) he would be dedicated to God from the womb, 2) he would be a Nazirite his entire life, and 3) he would begin to deliver his people from the Philistines.

These two God-fearing Danites would not have missed the implications of this threefold uniqueness. To begin with, dedication to the Lord from the womb had never been done before Samson. It was an honor given to only four people in the Bible: Samson, Samuel, John the Baptist, and Jesus. This is unique because the Law called for a firstborn male's dedication only *after* his mother's period of purification (Ex. 13:2; Lev. 12:2-6). Samson's dedication *from* the womb was something new and special indeed.

As previously covered, the Nazirite vow was a free-will vow, purposed by the individual; but this was not the case for Samson. He was to be a Nazirite his entire life beginning from his conception until the day of his death. He had no say in this calling. This too was special, being an exception and not the rule of the Nazirite vow.

And finally, Manoah and his wife were told their son would be the next in a long line of judges—a deliverer chosen by God to set His people free. Their hearts must have soared to consider that their son would follow in the footsteps of the legendary Ehud, Gideon, or Barak. This would be the equivalent of an angel telling you that your son was called of God to one day be the president or prime minister of your country. Imagine how your view of parenting would suddenly change.

No wonder, Manoah, his father, unlike any parent in the entire Bible record, requested specific instructions on how to raise this promised son. For such a special son, there must be more to his upbringing than Deuteronomy 6:6 and 7. The angel of God reaffirmed that Samson was to be raised a Nazirite from conception. His mother was commanded to sanctify herself her entire pregnancy by abstaining from any fruit of the vine. It appears Manoah and his wife completely honored the instructions of the Lord and Samson was reared to fulfill his divine calling as judge. And he did remain a Nazirite his entire life, even until death (his shaved head was not his doing but Delilah's).

It is also quite possible Samson was the fulfillment of Jacob's prophecy to his son Dan 555 years earlier in Genesis 49:16-18:

> **Dan shall judge his people, as one of the tribes of Israel. Dan shall be a serpent by the way, an adder in the path, that biteth the horse heels, so that his rider shall fall backward. I have waited for thy salvation, O LORD.**

Samson was a Danite judge who, like an adder, had his strength in his head, lethal even in death. When he struck, he didn't kill the horse but rather threw off the rider. He didn't destroy the Philistine kingdom, but he did begin to throw off their power.

It is no coincidence that Samson, the most unique of all the judges, is the final *shoftim* in the book of Judges. For 277 years, Israel was led by judges but to no lasting revival, long-term reform, or solidified victory. Israel refused to listen to their judges, even though the judges' ministries continuously afforded them deliverance and peace. Time and again the judges brought victory against the enemy and relief from their oppression, only to have Israel quickly return to the sins of idolatry and intermarriage. But one can see a different strategy purposed in the heart of God begin to emerge with the ministry of Samson.

Never before Samson had a Nazirite vow been commanded. Never before Samson had such power over an enemy been demonstrated through a single leader. I fully believe that the intention of God through Samson's ministry was to teach Israel that a lifestyle of consecration and devotion to Jehovah God, as demonstrated by a Nazirite judge, would result in power, victory, and deliverance for any and all who would follow suit. In essence, Samson's ministry was meant to be an advertisement for what Jehovah God could and would do through such a consecrated vessel. I believe Samson's life was meant to ignite a revival, in essence, producing a generation of Nazirites that would once and for all bring about Israel's total victory over the heathen nations still inhabiting the Promised Land.

This plan did ultimately produce a little fruit near the end of Samson's lifetime when a barren woman named Hannah entered the Tabernacle to seek God for a child. No doubt Hannah would have known the by-then famous story of Samson's miraculous conception and divine infant consecration. And, seeing the similarities between her situation and that of Samson's mother, Hannah made a Nazirite vow to God on behalf of the child she did not yet have but desired God to give her (1 Sam. 1:11). God granted her desire and Samuel was born the same year Samson died. Whereas Samson "*began* to deliver Israel out of the hands of the Philistines," Samuel *continued* Samson's work and subdued the Philistines, reclaiming lost land for Israel (1 Sam. 7:9-14).

Samson: A Type of Christ

Many theologians and preachers have pointed out the Christ-typology evident in the life of Samson. To be fair, all of the judges are arguably shadows of Jesus Christ as leaders who were raised up to deliver God's people from their oppressors. Of course, Christ-typology isn't just limited to the judges. Moses was a type of Christ as was Joseph, Joshua, Boaz, David, etc., each in their own unique way. Yet Samson's life had many uncanny parallels to Jesus Christ that are worth noting. Consider the following parallels between Samson and Christ:

- An angel divinely foretold their births.
- Both were dedicated to the Lord from the womb.
- They were born to deliver their people from their enemies.
- Their ministries totally frustrated their enemies.
- Samson's name is rooted in the Hebrew word for "Sun" and, like Jesus Christ, "the Sun of Righteousness," he arose to deliver his people (Mal. 4:2-3) and help them tread down the wicked.
- They were betrayed by close friends for the price of silver (Judas and Delilah).
- They were publicly mocked and ridiculed by their torturers.
- The power of their ministries increased until their deaths.
- Both cried out to God in the last moments of their lives.
- Their deaths were the greatest demonstration of their power.
- They died with arms stretched out: Christ on the cross, Samson between two pillars.
- Their bodies were collected from among their enemies and laid in private graves.

These parallels make Samson's failure even more unfortunate.

PART II
The Four Secrets of Samson's Destruction

Chapter 5

DESTRUCTIVE SECRET No.1-
Do Life and Ministry Alone

In the beginning, God made man and set him in His garden to tend it and keep it. That man, Adam, was sinless, innocent, and in daily fellowship with the Lord God. The total setting of Adam's existence, assignment, and fellowship with God was flawless. What could possibly be lacking? Yet God looked upon His creation and said something peculiar, "It is not good for the man to be alone: I will make a suitable helper for him." This raises an obvious question: how could the man be alone if he daily fellowshipped with God? What followed were the creation of woman and the institution of holy matrimony.

The Genesis account of man's "forming" and woman's "building"[12] is recorded for more than just historical purposes. In this account, God reveals His pattern for life, marriage, and ministry: a pattern of life because Adam's purpose was to serve in God's garden and fellowship with Him while doing it; a pattern of marriage because God brought the woman to Adam (he didn't have to leave serving God to find her); and a pattern of ministry because the purpose for woman's creation was to provide the man *companionship* and *help* in his garden ministry.

Much to some men's disappointment, the primary purpose for creating the woman was not sex. Sex was not at the forefront of anyone's mind here. Not Adam's because it hadn't been invented yet, and not

---

[12] The Hebrew uses two different words to describe Adam and Eve's creation. Man was *wayyitsar* or "formed," from the idea of "squeezing or molding into shape," while the woman was *wayyiven* or "built." This implies that God gave more attention to the creation of the woman.

God's because it's not one of the reasons He voiced for creating woman. (Sexual intimacy is a wonderful secondary benefit, but it was not the primary purpose here.) *Companionship* and *help* are the two principal things God Almighty declared man was lacking in the Garden of Eden *before* the Fall.

Even in the God-inhabited perfection of the Eden utopia, man simply wasn't designed to succeed alone. And, if, in the midst of sinless perfection man was never designed to operate alone, how much more do we need both companionship and help today?

No one is called to do life alone. Sadly enough though, this is one of Samson's enduring testimonies. Samson was a loner. He was called to judge Israel, but there is no record of him either settling disputes or administrating his people like Deborah did. Though Samson was called to be a leader, there is no biblical evidence he ever led anyone. We see no mention of him ever being surrounded by soldiers like Ehud, Gideon, Barak, or Jephthah were. We have no record of his children, nephews, or in-laws like the Bible records of Gideon, Jair, Ibzan, or Abdon. Furthermore, there is no evidence he was ever surrounded with elders like Joshua was, nor is there a record of an Israelite tribe ever requesting his help like in the case of Jephthah. Sure he was anointed, but he wasn't anointed to be a loner. He is presented as an anomaly among the judges—a vagabond beholden to no one but himself and his unrestrained desires.

Samson's social interactions can be summarized as either being *alone* in a remote place, being *alone* among God's enemies, or being *alone* with a pagan woman. His only intra-Israelite interaction, apart from his parents, occurred when 3,000 men from Judah visited him in his seclusion at the rock Etam to deliver him over to the Philistines. It is unfortunate that these men of Judah did not approach Samson for military leadership in order to overthrow the Philistines. No, quite the contrary! They came to arrest him and hand him over to the Philistines—their own oppressors.

It may be, that as famous as Samson had become in his day, part of his reputation was his lone-wolf *modus operandi*. For this reason, it's probable these men of Judah didn't bother to try and join Samson because he didn't need help, or, perhaps more likely, he didn't want help. More striking is that it doesn't even seem to have crossed Samson's mind to recruit these 3,000 men (or anyone else for that matter) to help him in what had become his one-man-war against the Philistines. We may never know what could have been accomplished had Samson recruited and trained these men to help him.

What about leadership in Samson's life? If he were a Moses, where was his Jethro? If he were a Joshua, where was his Moses? If he were a Samuel, where was his Eli? If he were a Saul, where was his Samuel? If he were a David, where was his Nathan? All of these great leaders had someone in their lives they trusted more than themselves. Even fearful and reluctant Barak had a Deborah he could look to for encouragement. Not Samson. Samson was a loner. The last voice of counsel in his life came from his parents pleading with him (from the Law of Moses) not to marry a heathen. Samson was a loner, and loners deprive themselves of the safety of wise counsel.

Samson's Lonely Track Record

Samson's solitary lifestyle was not something he slowly devolved into. Rather, it seems to have been his way of life from the beginning of his ministry. Judges 13:24-25 reveals that the Spirit of the Lord began to move (trouble) Samson as he grew up in a Danite[13] camp. Keep in mind this Danite camp was something of an emigrant's camp situated in the midst of Philistine territory (see Map 4, p.98). At this time, the Philistines still abode in their cities while the Danites had to dwell in tents. The Danites had been given this territory by God as an inheritance over 300 years prior, but had yet to fully occupy it and drive out the Philistines.

---

[13] Danites: Israelites from the tribe of Dan.

It is in this camp, *Mahaneh-Dan*, where the anointing and calling on Samson's life began to stir. Just as the calling of God upon Moses began to stir within him when he saw his people afflicted by the Egyptians, it is not difficult to imagine how the Spirit of the Lord would begin to impel and agitate a young Samson when he was in an emigrant's camp surrounded by the enemies of the Lord. Now imagine how much more the anointing to deliver might burn and compel the young judge—a judge whose calling was to destroy Philistines—when it was the Philistines he daily watched come and go, oppressing and abusing his people.

We don't know at what age this began, but it is safe to assume that it was no later than Samson's adolescence. Unfortunately, he had no one to turn to for guidance or discipleship as Samuel would later do when the prophet's anointing began to stir him as a young boy one generation later (1 Sam. 3:1-18). Certainly Eli's oversight and tutelage in Samuel's life was a tremendous factor in the boy-prophet's success. In contrast, Samson had no such mentor, so it appears he was left to grow alone in his calling.

His first foray against the Philistines involved his marriage to a Philistine woman from Timnath (Judges 14). Though his parents objected to this relationship from the Law of God, the Bible is clear that "the LORD was at work in this, creating an opportunity to work against the Philistines, who ruled over Israel at that time*"* (Judges 14:4 NLT). Though this interaction was of God, Samson was still alone at his own wedding, and ultimately, the marriage was never consummated. The only Israelites present were his parents. In fact, the bride's family had to provide men to stand with Samson as his groomsmen.

"As his father was making final arrangements for the marriage, Samson threw a party at Timnath, as was the custom for elite young men. When the bride's parents saw him, they selected thirty young men from the town to be his companions" (Judges 14:10-11 NLT). What kind of man doesn't even have a friend to stand with him at his own engagement party? His groomsmen were 30 Philistines, 30 of Israel's enemies, provided by the Philistine bride's family. Samson was a loner at his own wedding.

When the answer to his famous riddle was surreptitiously answered by his Philistine groomsmen, Samson was obligated to keep his word and provide them with 30 sets of garments. Samson traveled *alone* to the coastal city of Ashkelon and there, empowered by the Holy Spirit but still *alone*, he slew 30 Philistines and took their garments as payment.

Samson's retribution against the Philistines for giving his wife to another man was to burn the local crops down. This act of revenge was carried out *alone*. Samson caught 300 foxes and tied their tails together *alone*. He tied firebrands to their tails *alone*. He lit the firebrands and strategically released them *alone*, burning down their corn, grapes, and olive crops. In retribution, the Philistines burned Samson's wife and family alive. Samson's next act of vengeance was also carried out *alone*. And *alone* he smote them "hip and thigh," or "with a cruel and unsparing slaughter."[14]

He then retreated to live in *solitude* at the rock Etam, only to be delivered up by his fellow Israelites into the hands of the Philistines. It is there at Lehi, with the "jaw of an ass," that Samson smote a thousand Philistines *alone*, without anyone to help or to share in the victory celebration.

Samson then travelled to Gaza *alone* and met a harlot. The Gazites[15] surrounded the city in order to take him. Once again, he arose *alone*, accomplished a tremendous miracle of strength *alone*, and fled *alone*.

And finally, when the wiles and continuous pressing of Delilah had bested Samson, he was *alone* when he was taken, no fellow Danite or Hebrew in sight. He was in the enemy's territory and in the enemy's bed. He was *alone* when they put out his eyes and *alone* when they made him to grind at the mill. He is recorded as being the *lone* entertainment at the great feast of Dagon—a feast celebrating his own

---

[14] Keil and Delitzsch, *Commentary of the Old Testament,* Vol. 2, 414.

[15] Philistines from Gaza.

defeat. Fitting enough, even in his death, he was *alone* without a fellow Israelite in sight. He died just as he lived—*alone*! It is only after his death that his fellow Danites and his family were able to enter back into the picture. They retrieved his body from the ruins of Dagon's destroyed temple and buried him with his father, Manoah.

Modern "Samsons"

Many Christians and ministers today are just like Samson. Genuinely anointed of God but convinced they can serve God all alone. For whatever reason, people become convinced they can do life alone. Nobody is called to do life alone. Nobody is called to be alone and nobody is able to succeed alone. Hermits can hardly be called a success story. The crotchety old recluse never masters life and, sadly, usually dies alone and without notice. The bitter curmudgeon barely makes a ripple in the ocean of life as he sinks into nameless oblivion. God has designed each member of the Body of Christ to need the other members. Each member possesses gifts, graces, and abilities that are lacking in the other members. In this manner, God has designed us to require the rest of the Body of Christ to succeed.

The New Testament teaches us that we are each members of a body—the Body of Christ. We have been set in that Body where it has pleased God (1 Cor. 12:18-25), and He will never set us off somewhere alone. Paul also stated we are a "building fitly framed *together*" (Eph. 2:19-22) and a "body fitly joined *together*" (Eph. 4:16). Whether a body or a building, we can only succeed together. Too many believers have chosen to be a lone piece of lumber or an amputated hand.

Those who go it alone end up failing alone, and they usually die alone—just like Samson. This is why God has given every Christian the gift of the local church. Every Christian belongs in a local church. It is there you will find fellowship with people of like faith. You will find accountability and protection. You will find rest and spiritual nourishment for your soul. You will also find the oversight of a local shepherd. There is absolutely no reason for a Christian to ever feel alone in life. Every Christian must find a local church that will give them the Word of God and the fellowship of the saints!

The Body of Christ is also referred to as a family. The New Testament is full of terms describing our spiritual family. When God revealed Himself as *The* Father, He was painting for us the picture of family. Being born-again gives you a new Father and a new big brother (Jesus Christ—He's not ashamed to call us brethren, Heb. 2:11). We have fathers and mothers in the faith and we entreat one another as siblings. If you are a born-again believer, you are part of an eternal family.

> **For this cause I bow my knees unto the Father of our Lord Jesus Christ, Of whom the whole family in heaven and earth is named,   Ephesians 3:14-15**

> **God setteth the solitary (lonely) in families: he bringeth out those which are bound with chains: but the rebellious dwell in a dry land.   Psalm 68:6**

We are designed to be part of a family. God sets the solitary and the lonely into a family. Psalm 68:6 concludes by saying rebellious people live in a dry land. Living life alone can certainly be described as a dry land. It is not God's will for you to be rebellious and dwell in desolate isolation.

Even non-believers have within them the desire to seek out family. They create family units called clubs, fraternities, sororities, associations, and brotherhoods. Mankind gathers to these assemblies in order to share life, find meaning, enjoy protection, and develop relationships. God has given us His family—Christ's Body—the local church family. No Christian ever needs to experience loneliness or isolation. You have been given a family!

Ministry "Samsons"

Likewise, no minister is designed to labor alone. Ministry by default is lonely. Ministers need the fellowship of other ministers. They need the oversight of spiritual fathers, mentors, and yes, even a pastor. Ministers are unique because they are twice called-out. First when they are born-again, being called out of darkness into the glorious light of the Gospel, and then a second time when they are called out from the Body of Christ into an office of full time ministry to lead the Body.

Ministry can and will literally suck the life right out of you. The spiritual demands upon a minister are staggering. This higher calling places the minister in a lonely and unique place. The gospel minister is anointed by God to help God's people, but he or she is not anointed to help him or herself.

Hear me very clearly, dear minister, you don't have a special anointing for yourself. You are only anointed for God's people. You must deal with your private life like every other Christian must: through prayer, fasting, sacrifice, and discipline. You must sit under other anointed ministers to receive the same life-changing benefits others receive from you. It is for this reason the Gospel minister must seek out fellowship, accountability, and oversight. The Gospel minister was never meant to be a loner or a vagabond. Isolationism has been the cause of many ministry implosions.

Submission, Fellowship, and Help

The Bible presents a very clear recipe for success in life. It's quite simple but requires great humility. The arrogant will have every excuse why they don't have to abide by it, but the Bible pattern holds true. If you want to enjoy biblical success and avoid repeating Samson's shortcomings, you'll need to incorporate the necessary ingredients of *submission, fellowship,* and *help* into your life: *submitting* to those who have the rule over you, *fellowshipping* with those of like precious faith, and asking for *help* when you need it. Sticking to this simple recipe will almost certainly guarantee your success in the Kingdom of God.

Moses

The great leaders of the Bible followed this recipe in their life. Moses, the humblest of men, submitted to a spiritual father (in-law), Jethro, the high priest of Midia (Ex. 18:7-27). Moses didn't lead Israel by himself. He was humble enough to ask for and receive help when he needed it. Moses also had Aaron his brother as an interpreter (Ex. 4:10-17). Aaron and Hur served as support staff (literally) to Moses during one particularly arduous battle against the Amalekites (Ex. 17:8-16). Joshua served as Moses's military general and servant (Ex. 17:9-11). As Moses's ministry and vision grew, he had to have more help. He cried out to God, and God gave him judges to help bear the burdens of the people's problems (Ex. 18:13-26) and elders to help bear the responsibilities (Num. 11:10-30).

Moses wasn't a loner. He fellowshipped with righteous people, and he was aided by Jethro, Aaron, Hur, Joshua, the 70 elders, and the 120 judges. That's six levels of help. Without debate, Moses was one of the greatest men in the Bible!

David

David's early life was submitted to first his father Jesse, then King Saul, and later to the prophets and priests who provided correction, wisdom, and direction. After his appointment as king, 400 men and families gathered to David in the Cave Adullam. That number grew to 600 men. From those men, David trained and promoted his mighty men of valor. After becoming king, David wisely surrounded himself with many advisors and subordinates who helped him administrate his kingdom. Following the recipe of *submission*, *fellowship*, and *help,* David's might and influence knew no bounds.

However, there came a terrible day when Israel's greatest king chose to isolate himself and reject help. In doing so, he mired his legacy and brought a sword upon his household. "At the time when kings go forth to battle, . . . David tarried still at Jerusalem" (2 Sam. 11:1). He stayed behind when all his leadership and accountability marched off to war.

That isolation afforded him time alone with Bathsheba, resulting in her pregnancy and an attempted cover-up. When the cover-up failed, David had Uriah, Bathsheba's husband, moved to the front lines of battle to ensure his death.

David's sinful conspiracy invoked God's judgment upon his household, which ultimately resulted in the death of four of his sons.[16] His act of isolation did what no enemy nation or army could do—it brought his flourishing kingdom to a screeching halt. Absalom, his own son, challenged his throne and moved to steal Israel away from him. His most trusted counselor Ahithophel betrayed him and advised Absalom to publicly sleep with some of his father's wives (2 Sam. 16:20-23). What a disaster. David recovered his throne, but just barely, and the last 20 years of his reign paled in comparison to the glory of his first 20 years.

David excelled when he wasn't alone. His one act of isolation soiled his legacy. Don't set yourself up for failure like David. Don't isolate yourself. Don't be a loner.

Childlike Faith

The Bible is filled with countless others who succeeded—not alone—but *submitted* to leaders, *fellowshipping* with other servants, and with the *help* of others. King Jehoash pleased God "all the days in which Jehoida the priest instructed him" (2 Kings 12:2). This king wasn't too prideful to submit to the priest, learn, and get help. Then again, he was a seven-year-old boy when he became king, so perhaps submission to the priest came naturally for him; however, we can never use our adult status as an excuse.

Jesus taught that we must become as a child if we want to inherit the kingdom. You may no longer be a child, but you must always maintain childlike faith. Childlike faith doesn't have a problem asking for help. It

---

[16] David's rash response to the prophet Nathan's "little lamb" story demanded the fourfold restoration of the poor man's sheep. David was judged by his own words and it cost him four sons for the life of Uriah: 1) Bathsheba's illegitimate child died of sickness, 2) Absalom murdered Amnon, 3) Joab killed Absalom, 4) Solomon killed Adonijah.

doesn't have trouble looking up to leaders. You may be an old man or woman now with your childhood decades behind you, but "truly I tell you, unless you change and become like little children, you will never enter the kingdom of heaven. Therefore, whoever takes the lowly position of the child is the greatest in the kingdom of heaven" (Matt. 18:3-4 NIV). Childlike faith doesn't have a problem being told what to do by someone in authority.

Jesus

Ultimately, we have no greater example than our Savior. Jesus wasn't a loner. He had 12 disciples, then a contingency of 70 more disciples. When He sent the 12 out, He didn't send them out alone, but together in pairs. The disciples were *submitted* to their master, *fellowshipping* with each other, and getting *help* when they needed it (Luke 5:6-7). Truthfully, a lifestyle of submission and fellowship will automatically produce an atmosphere where spiritual help is constantly and readily available. If Jesus wasn't a loner, are we better than our Master?

The Early Church

The early Church had a strong doctrine of submission and fellowship. It was necessary for their encouragement and survival.

> **So then, those who had received his word were baptized; and that day there were added about three thousand souls. They were continually devoting themselves to the apostles' teaching and to fellowship, to the breaking of bread and to prayer.**
>
> **Acts 2:41-42 NASB**

The early Christians weren't just devoted to Bible study and prayer; they were devoted to the apostles' teachings. This speaks of their *submission* to their church leaders. They were also devoted to *fellowship*, which shows their desire to open up and share their lives with others. They didn't just come a little late to church and then leave a little early, never getting to know their brothers and sisters in Christ. They were actually invested in one another. They understood how important it was (and still is) to submit to someone greater than themselves and fellowship with one another. It is so critical that we learn to share our lives with the Body of Christ. If you don't learn to fellowship with the Body and serve God together, what will you do when your life is attacked?

The apostles lived by this rule as well. In Acts 4, Peter and John went up to the temple together. God used them to heal the impotent man at the Beautiful Gate. This miracle kicked off both a revival and a season of persecution for the apostles. Peter and John were arrested and imprisoned overnight. The next day they were interrogated by the biggest of the bigwigs, the heaviest of the heavy hitters—a veritable "who's who" among the religious ruling class. Present were the synagogue rulers, the elders of Israel, the scribes, Annas the high priest, Caiaphas (the high priest when the Lord was crucified), and all the kindred of the high priest. This was the group responsible for crucifying Jesus. Imagine the suffocating antichrist presence in that council chamber. In the end, Peter and John were thoroughly berated, threatened, and then released.

> **And being let go, <u>they went to their own company</u>, and reported all that the chief priests and elders had said unto them.**   **Acts 4:23**

The apostles had a company to go to in hard times. It was their default place of refuge. They didn't retreat to their private homes to lick their wounds and tremble in fear alone. No! They returned to their company— their church family—and they informed the believers of what happened to them. Immediately, a prayer service broke out that climaxed with a supernatural earthquake and the Holy Spirit refilling all those who were present, imparting a divine boldness.

Do you have a company? If not, what do you do when you're under attack? Where do you go when the enemy is threatening you? Having a company will help keep you filled with the Spirit and impart boldness into your Christian walk. God wants us to have a body of believers we can retreat to when the enemy rises against us.

The Apostle Paul

The Apostle Paul didn't do ministry alone. He travelled and ministered with a large group of disciples and fellow laborers. He was submitted to the church elders at Jerusalem and was always part of some kind of ministry partnership, whether it was "Barnabus and Saul" or "Paul and Silas." Even in prison he was never alone. At the end of his life he still had the "beloved physician" Luke with him (2 Tim. 4:11), and he requested the companionship and help of John Mark and Timothy.

Modern Loners

I have known pastors who were all alone in their pastorate. They lived for God's people but refused to submit to a spiritual father or pastor, some even resisting fellowship with other minsters. And why? Fear? Insecurity? Paranoia? Pride? Competition? Superiority? There are no good reasons to withdraw as a Gospel minister. Who will these pastors turn to for help when their church is attacked or when their marriage is under assault? Who do these leaders look to for aid, encouragement, or wisdom? Sadly, there will be no help for them in time of need. Because they have no one over them in ministry, there will be no one to pull them up when they fall. And because they have no friend near them, there will be no one of equal measure to lend them a hand or an encouraging word in time of need.

Missionary "Samsons"

Likewise, I have met missionaries who are all alone on the mission field. No one sent them out, so no one knows where they are. Sure, mom and dad might know where they are, but no one with any sort of Kingdom authority knows they're out there playing missionary. One great missionary of 30-plus years said, "Successful missionary work is like building a bridge. You must have a great foundation *sending* the missionary and a great foundation *receiving* the missionary. And if you don't have both, the bridge will collapse." Unfortunately, many missionaries do collapse because they lack oversight, accountability, and a spiritual covering. In fact, our dear missionaries in East Africa reported that they witnessed 54 missionary families withdraw from the mission field in less than six years. The most common factor observed was their lack of pastoral support and proper New Testament send off.[17] Where is their encouragement in time of discouragement? Where is their help in time of need? They are prime candidates for ministry burnout or sinful implosion. Consider the wisdom of what Ecclesiastes 4:9-12 says:

> **Two are better than one; because they have a good reward for their labour. For if they fall, the one will lift up his fellow: but woe to him that is alone when he falleth; for he hath not another to help him up. Again, if two lie together, then they have heat: but how can one be warm alone? And if one prevail against him, two shall withstand him; and a threefold cord is not quickly broken.   Ecclesiastes 4:9-12**

The Body of Christ needs you and you need the Body of Christ. Don't withdraw yourself. Don't go through life alone. Samson's isolation ensured that he never had any accountability in his life. He never had anyone to tell him when he was wrong. Without any oversight in his life, he was free to flirt with the sin that would be his demise! Submit. Fellowship. Get help when you need it. Don't be like Samson! Don't do life alone and don't die alone.

---

[17] Paul and Barnabas established the biblical protocol for launching ministries in Acts 13:1-3. The leaders at the Antioch church were led by the Holy Spirit to separate Barnabas and Saul for their fledgling missionary ministry. Very few missionaries are sent off this way anymore. As one great preacher observed, "Some were sent, and some just went." Needless to say, those who "just went" usually experience ministry failure.

Chapter 6

DESTRUCTIVE SECRET No.2-
Flirt with Sin

Every nation and people group has its own culture. Culture is made up of morays, customs, taboos, mindsets, traditions, and even sins. Every people group has its own familiar sins. From the time of Othniel the first judge, the two great familiar sins of Israel were the intermarrying of Canaanites and the worship of their Baals and Asherahs. The Lord gave numerous warnings concerning these two major sins.

> **And when the LORD thy God shall deliver them before thee; thou shalt smite them, and utterly destroy them; thou shalt make no covenant with them, nor shew mercy unto them: Neither shalt thou make marriages with them; thy daughter thou shalt not give unto his son, nor his daughter shalt thou take unto thy son. For they will turn away thy son from following me, that they may serve other gods: so will the anger of the LORD be kindled against you, and destroy thee suddenly.**
>
> **Deuteronomy 7:2-4**
>
> **(See also Ex. 23:32-33; 34:12; Deut. 7:16; Josh. 23:7-8; Judges 2:2; 3:6)**

As an Israelite, Samson would have been ever mindful of his people's national sins. As the 13th judge, he would have been more than familiar with the cycle of sin and oppression experienced by Israel in this season of their history. He would have known his people's weaknesses, just as ministers today should be ever mindful of their nation's sins and even their own church's familiar transgressions.

Israel was constantly facing defeat, oppression, and subjugation due to these two habitual acts of rebellion. These two national sins were also the reason why God raised up judges like Samson. Samson was anointed to deliver his people from their enemies, leading them out of their rebellious lifestyle and into paths of righteousness. However, in the end, Samson succumbed to some of the same sins.

Though he never dabbled in the idolatry of the Philistines, he is best known for his illicit relationships with Philistine women. For one of God's leaders to so recklessly and foolishly play on the banks of national sin is unthinkable. How could he trifle with the very sin he was called to lead people out of? Simply put, Samson was a fool to flirt with Philistine women when it was one of the major transgressions that had repeatedly cursed Israel for nearly 300 years.

A Pattern of Perversion

One of the patterns that arises in the life of Samson is the increase in his sinful compromise. To put it succinctly, he *enjoyed* flirting with sin. As is evident from the Bible narrative, when Samson should have been growing cleaner, holier, and more influential, his private life was, in fact, growing increasingly sinful. His relationship with women demonstrated this doomed trajectory.

His first love was a Philistine woman from Timnath. Though he was honorable with the Timnite woman, the marriage was destined to fail. The Law of Moses strictly forbade intermarrying the inhabitants of the land. The Bible is clear: this particular relationship was a means by which the Lord sought occasion against the Philistines (Judges 14:4).

The second Philistine woman in Samson's life was a harlot with whom he should never have had an encounter. Whereas Samson had an actual relationship with the first Philistine woman, this was nothing but a perverse one-night stand. This event revealed Samson's recklessness and increased callousness to sin. The Bible brusquely describes the stereotypical encounter "johns" and hookers have been having for thousands of years, "Then went Samson to Gaza, and saw there an harlot, and went in unto her" (Judges 16:1). Samson saw a harlot and had sex with her. It was as simple as that. Oh, how sin cheapens what God has designed to be precious and priceless.

Not only was this fornication, it was fornication with a Philistine. And not just a Philistine, but a Philistine prostitute. No single action seems to demonstrate such a lack of morality, self-respect, or restraint quite like paying to have sex with a total stranger. What better way to say "I'm submitted to no man, no law, no restraint. I am my own man, beholden to none" than to sleep with a harlot. Yet this was where flirting with sin was slowly taking our legendary judge.

The first Philistine he intended to marry because he loved her. The second Philistine he used to satisfy an animalistic appetite. The third Philistine woman would be a combination of the two. His final encounter with a Philistine woman was his undoing. As previously discussed, God had commanded Israel to abstain from seeking the peace or prosperity of any heathen "all thy days for ever" (Deut. 23:6). Samson willfully violated this law (and others) in order to pursue Delilah. Once he had established his unlawful love for her in his heart, fornication was the next natural step towards destruction.

Samson's sex with Delilah was bizarre and perverse. We must be honest, only a sexual setting and "pillow talk" sets the stage for a man to fabricate "secrets to his strength" requiring him to be tied up in numerous outlandish scenarios. He mistook her treacherous inquiries as an opportunity to engage in his perverse fetishes. He could have answered her questions with any number of lies, but he didn't. Things could have unfolded like this:

Delilah: "Samson, my love, what is the secret to your strength?"
Samson: "If I eat any unclean food I will become as a normal man."
Delilah: "Really?!"

Samson: "Okay, seriously, if I wear the sandals of a Gentile, I shall
be as any man."

Delilah: "Seriously? Please don't lie to me."

Samson: "Alas, if I bathe in the milk of a kid of the goats, my
strength shall depart me."

Each of these could have just as easily been tested and proven to be a ruse, but no! All of Samson's lies involved binding scenarios. He used her questions to further facilitate his sexual fantasies—perversions he developed by flirting with sin. How else can you explain a mighty Israelite warrior allowing himself to be tied up three times in a row, only to have the Philistines rush in each time, and yet never grow suspicious of his lover's next round of questioning?

Never did the coincidence of their intimate talks followed by a Philistine attack cross his mind. Never did it dawn on him that she was the bait and a trap was slowly being set. As the late Dr. Lester Sumrall was fond of saying, "Sin will make you stupid." Perhaps I should have entitled this book: *Samson: Mighty but Stupid!*

Samson's flirtation with sin eventually cost him his consecration. Once his consecration was gone, so was his power. Consecration was the secret to his power, just as it is for Christians today. No consecration, no power. There is something absolutely unstoppable about a holy, consecrated believer. There is also an intimidating boldness that belongs only to the clean, consecrated servant of God. Dirty Christians will never have nor understand holy boldness.

A Forfeited Consecration

Samson didn't forfeit his consecration overnight and neither do Christians. We forfeit our consecration by means of a slow and steady process of flirting with our familiar sins. By familiar sins, I mean those sins that are unique and habitual to each one of us. They are the sins that we seem to struggle with over and over again. These are the trespasses we've beaten a path to time and time again, and therefore, we are comfortable and familiar with them.

We have yet to suffer any catastrophic loss at the hands of these sins, so we dangerously tolerate their existence in our lives. We cannot forget that sin always pays wages—and that wage is death! Willfully sinning is like playing a scratch-off ticket—you never know what you'll uncover. We gamble with our lives when we play with our pet sins rather than put them to death (Rom. 8:13). We never know when sin will issue its paycheck. For Samson, sin cost him the anointing of God and he "did not know that the LORD was departed from him." How utterly terrifying!

Eye Problems

Samson's habitual sins were his wandering eyes and his sexual appetites, and the one gave way to the other. It's curious how the Bible repeatedly references Samson's visual appetites:

> **And Samson went down to Timnath, and <u>saw a woman</u> in Timnath of the daughters of the Philistines.   Judges 14:1**

> **And he came up, and told his father and his mother, and said, <u>I have seen a woman</u> in Timnath of the daughters of the Philistines: now therefore get her for me to wife.   Judges 14:2**

> **Then went Samson to Gaza, and <u>saw there an harlot</u>, and went in unto her.   Judges 16:1**

No doubt, like many men, Samson had a wandering eye problem. Over time, what started as simply noticing a pretty girl here or there grew into full-fledged sexual leering. Those unrestrained leers led to sexual sin and eventually his downfall. How cruel an irony his demise: the only physical injury his enemies were ever able to inflict upon him was the gouging out of his eyes. Never again would Samson be able to see a beautiful woman, a beautiful sunset, or even the temple he was to die in. The short time he had left was spent in total darkness.

Jesus, perhaps recalling Samson's fate and desirous of His followers to avoid a similar fate, admonished His disciples to put out their own eyes if they were a source of offense. The very sin we refuse to deal with today will always grow up to deal with us harshly later. Weeds are always easier to pull up when they are small and tender. But just ignore weeds for a season or two, and the next thing you know, you will need a chain saw or tractor to eliminate the unwanted growth. Samson discovered all too late that you cannot safely flirt with sin. He learned how deceptive sin could be.

The Deceitfulness of Sin

But exhort one another daily, while it is called To day; lest any of you be hardened through the <u>deceitfulness of sin</u>.   Hebrews 3:13

Sin is deceitful. It subtly hardens a person's heart. The *hardening* mentioned in this verse has a two-fold application. First, if someone has been hardened by sin, they are stubborn and obstinate. They refuse to quit sinning. The book of Jeremiah likens this stubborn attitude to having "a whore's forehead," and one that "refusedst to be ashamed" (3:3). Jeremiah also describes a sinful, calloused heart as being so hard it can be engraved upon with a pen of iron (17:1).

The second application of *hardening* describes the callousing effect sin has on the transgressor's heart. Sin will callous your heart, thereby slowly hardening it. We should all be familiar with the natural callouses that can form on our hands or feet. If we look at the formation of these natural callouses we can learn a lot about the beguiling effects of sin.

Natural callouses aren't formed with the first exposure to friction, nor are they formed overnight. Callouses take a lot of work to form and require consistent and regular application of friction or pressure to the skin. Often the first exposure of friction or pressure results in pain and regret. The timid might retreat while the determined will press on.

Guitar players develop callouses on the tips of their fingers from regularly playing their guitar. These callouses insulate the musician from the pain of constantly pressing against the guitar strings, allowing them to play longer and longer.

Weightlifters develop callouses on the palms of their hands from regularly lifting weights. These callouses insulate the weightlifter from the pain of their hands constantly rubbing against bars and weights, allowing them to lift heavier and longer.

Likewise, high mileage runners can develop callouses on their feet and toes. These callouses insulate their feet from the pain of blister-producing friction, allowing them to run even greater distances.

Humans can develop callouses on their heart and soul from habitually sinning. These callouses aren't developed overnight but by the constant, long-term exposure to and practice of sin. Spiritual callouses insulate the individual from the pain of their rebellion, allowing them to sin in even more egregious and wicked ways – even possibly pioneering new sin.

Sin is also deceitful because it feels good to the flesh for a season (though it does rub the pious, pure conscience raw at first) while rarely bringing immediate consequences. It is a dangerous game of roulette when an intelligent believer knows their actions are sinful, but they begin to reason, "It feels good and it hasn't cost me anything yet, so . . . I'm safe to do it again. And I can always repent later."

Sin is deceitful because it usually starts off small, seemingly innocuous, and easily justifiable. To be clear, not every sinful act has an immediate and noticeable effect, but we know the wages of sin is death because God has said so. In this regard, sin is a lot like any number of toxic chemicals. It may appear that your body can safely consume and process small amounts of toxin, but make no mistake about it, there is internal damage inflicted every time even the smallest amount of poison is consumed. Eventually, you will reach a saturation point where organs begin to shut down and the body fails.

The wages of sin is death, but even in the natural a paycheck takes time to accumulate. You can work for 15 minutes, and though technically you have earned a fraction of an hourly or weekly rate, the earned wage doesn't warrant a paycheck . . . yet. But if you keep working, the earned wage grows. Justice requires a paycheck be issued. This is great if we're talking about finances; this is painful when it's sin. You can keep chasing sin if you want, but let me reiterate—all sin has a paycheck! That paycheck is death, and though death may come in numerous denominations, it's still death.

The Little Foxes

Song of Solomon makes an interesting observation about foxes and how they can ruin a vineyard in bloom:

> **Catch the foxes for us, The little foxes that are ruining the vineyards, While our vineyards are in blossom.   Song of Solomon 2:15 NASB**

This famous verse of poetry produces such an amazing portrait of sin and its stratagems in our Christian walk. Our lives are like a beautiful vineyard in bloom, flowering right before we bring forth precious fruit. Our lives also possess hedges of protection designed to provide peace and safety, just like the vineyards in biblical times. These ancient hedges were typically literal hedges of thorn bushes planted simultaneously with the vineyard. As the vines developed, so did the hedge of protection. The thorn bushes grew up, their thorns crisscrossed, and their growth produced an impenetrable barrier designed to keep out every type of vermin.

The only threat was a sly, little fox. A large fox was not a problem because the hedge of thorns gave no access for the full-bodied enemy. But the little foxes – so cute, so cuddly, and so seemingly playful – they were the vermin that could find the tiniest opening between the barbed branches and prickly nettles. It was there, in that tiny opening, that a little adorable fox was able to gain access into the vineyard and begin to dig at the roots and eat the fruit.

As if this wasn't bad enough, as the little fox would come and go from the vineyard, it inadvertently made its little hole larger, breaking off the occasional briar, thorn, and branch. The enlarged hole made way for a slightly larger fox, who in turn did more damage by eating more grapes, digging more holes, chewing at more roots, and upon exiting, enlarging the hole a little more. Before long, every fox in the area had been afforded free access to the vineyard. It was only a matter of time before the once beautiful and fruitful vineyard became nothing but a dead vine surrounded by thorns and thistles.

So it is with sin and its desire to access the vineyard of our life. As the Lord admonished Cain, "sin is crouching at the door; and its desire is for you, but you must master it" (Gen. 4:7 NASB). Sin patrols our perimeter looking for access into our lives and, more often than not, seems to find an entrance. It lies at the door, but we must master it. We often justify the comings and goings of this sin because we see it as a "cute little fox" of a sin and "what possible harm could come of its presence?" The Bible gives the imperative: catch the fox! Don't play with it. Catch it and eliminate the threat before it opens your life and ruins your vineyard.

Warnings About Sin

I'm not sure today's believers are any smarter than Samson was. Christians continue to flirt with their own sins, convinced that it's not hurting them just because it hasn't cost them anything . . . yet. The Bible has many strong warnings concerning sin. In fact, sin, not the devil, is our mortal enemy. The devil is not always present, but lust and temptation are. Preachers should confront sin just as passionately and regularly as doctors confront sickness, police officers confront crime, and teachers confront ignorance. Any preacher who doesn't regularly preach against sin is derelict in their duties and quite possibly a man-pleaser. James 1:14-15 describes the infernal mechanics of sin:

> **But every man is tempted, when he is drawn away of his own lust, and enticed. Then when lust hath conceived, it bringeth forth sin: and sin, when it is finished (fully grown), bringeth forth death.**

James reveals the progression of a slippery slope that begins with an inward lust and culminates in death. Every person has inward lust, but not all lust is sexual. Lust is any illicit desire for something that God's Word forbids. Inward lust can produce a continuous internal enticement tempting the individual. If that temptation is yielded to, the resulting action will always be sin. If the original inward lust is not dealt with, the resulting lifestyle of sin will ultimately produce death. Preaching against sin both reminds and warns God's people to resist the inward impulses of their sin nature. It takes faith to resist temptation, and faith comes by hearing (and hearing and hearing). Christians need to constantly be reminded that God still views sin the same way He always has. They also need to hear that sin still destroys lives.

The wages of sin is death, but not all death results in a funeral and a tombstone. Some sin produces a death called divorce. Other sins produce a death called poverty. Sometimes sin produces a death called loneliness. Not all death is the instant cessation of natural life. Sometimes death keeps you alive but makes your life so miserable you wish you were dead.

Rather than flirt with sin, Paul exhorts us to "awake to righteousness, and sin not" (1 Cor. 15:34) and to abstain from anything that even remotely looks like sin (1 Thes. 5:22). The victorious Christian walk can be summarized by these two verses: stay awake and stay away from anything that appears to be evil. I think that's pretty simple.

Hebrews offers several warnings debunking any would-be-cavalier approach to sin:

> **Let us lay aside every weight, and <u>the sin which doth
> so easily beset us</u>, and let us run with patience the
> race that is set before us,   Hebrews 12:1**

Sin doesn't just beset us; it *easily* besets us. Hebrews warns us that sin is *besetting*, that is, it assails and attacks from every side.   Another translation of *beset* states that sin "entangles and acts like a thwarting competitor, trying to trip you at every step." Our destiny in Christ is a race we must run every day of our lives until we cross the finish line. Samson never finished his race. His sin tripped him up and caused him to fall into slavery. His sin literally blinded him, literally bound him (to a millstone), and literally caused him to go in circles (grinding corn) the rest of his life. That describes too many Christians I've tried to pastor over the years—blind, bound, and going in circles.

> **Ye have not yet resisted unto blood, striving against
> sin.   Hebrews 12:4**

Victory over sin requires a fight, a resistance, and strife. This verse implies that our fight against sin could even lead to bloodshed. What could Samson have become if he fought against sin like he did against the Philistines? What greater miracles and deliverances could God have accomplished through this Nazirite had he stayed consecrated?

For, "The one who desires life, to love and see good days, must keep his tongue from evil and his lips from speaking deceit. He must turn away from evil and do good; He must seek peace and pursuit it. For the eyes of the Lord are toward the righteous, and his ears attend to their prayer, <u>but the face of the Lord is against those who do evil</u>."   1 Peter 3:10-12 NASB

This passage, quoting from Psalms, juxtaposes good and evil three times. Peter implores us to take action against sin, not flirt with it. We are commanded to 1) keep our tongue from evil, 2) turn away from evil, and 3) seek peace and pursue it. Otherwise, the face of the Lord will be against us. The contrast between good and evil is also clearly revealed in Deuteronomy:

See, I have set before thee this day life and good, and death and evil;   Deuteronomy 30:15

This is the most basic of all evaluations of sin. Serving God is black and white. Every day we have two options set before us. Behavior is either sinful or it's righteous. If it's sinful, it will produce death and evil. Righteous behavior will produce life and goodness. Deuteronomy continues:

I call heaven and earth to record this day against you, that I have set before you life and death, blessing and cursing: therefore choose life, that both thou and thy seed may live. That thou mayest love the LORD thy God, and that thou mayest obey his voice, and that thou mayest cleave unto him: for he is thy life, and the length of thy days: that thou mayest dwell in the land

which the LORD sware unto thy fathers, to Abraham,
to Isaac, and to Jacob, to give them.
Deuteronomy 30:19-20

The Bible elaborates upon its description of sin versus obedience. Obedience to God's word brings blessing, life, length of days, and fulfillment of God's long-term promises in your life. Obedience begins with a choice: choose life.

Choosing the life of God will help you to love the Lord. Loving the Lord is followed by obeying the Lord and then cleaving unto the Lord. Evidently, we cannot say we love the Lord without obeying Him and cleaving to Him. Jesus taught the same thing: "If ye love me, keep my commandments" (John 14:15; 1 John 5:3).

Too many Christians seem to think they only have to love God with their mouths and not with their actions (Mark 7:6; 1 John 3:18). Please understand very clearly, just because you *say* you love God doesn't mean you actually *do*. No one would dare say they hated God, at least not any sane or rational person. God is looking for more than just a confession of your love. He is looking for a lifestyle that proves to Him and all the world that you actually do love Him. If you love God, you will cleave to Him and obey Him. If you claim to love Jesus, prove it by keeping His commandments.

Judas Flirted With Sin

If we could award a trophy to "Worst Person in the Bible," besides satan, the trophy would have to go to Judas Iscariot. His name has become synonymous with *traitor*, *betrayer,* and *scoundrel*. Even pagans can't stand a Judas. Though he may be most famous for his final acts of sin – the betrayal, the 30 pieces of silver, and his suicide by hanging – these actions were merely the climax of his private lifestyle of flirting with sin.

I'm sure all 12 of the Apostles of the Lamb, from Peter to Bartholomew, brought some kind of familiar sin and personality defect to the ministry when the Lord called them; how could they not? But while the other disciples demonstrated change and improvement with the one-on-one personal discipleship the Son of God gave them on a daily basis, Judas did not. Judas, like Samson, was mightily used by God on a regular basis but actually managed to somehow multiply his sinfulness with Jesus present.

How did Judas become the son of perdition? How did Judas come to a place where he could possibly think it was acceptable to betray the Savior? How? He flirted with his own familiar sin for over three years, that's how. He flirted with a sin he made no attempt to master. And what was the familiar sin he visited time and time again? What was the little fox that slowly pried open the door and allowed satan to enter his life? Petty theft. Judas embezzled money, and he did it from the beginning of the Lord's ministry (John 12:6).

The New American Standard Bible says Judas "pilfered" money from the ministry—that means he'd take a little money here and then maybe take a little money there. Perhaps he would use the Lord's almsgiving to the poor as a cover to pilfer and embezzle even more money than usual; after all, who's going to know what money went where? Regardless of what it looked like, the Bible is clear; Judas was a thief way before he was ever a traitor. But I suppose it could easily be argued that stealing from someone is the same thing as betraying them.

What follows is my personal opinion concerning the motives and machinations of Judas' betrayal. There are many thoughts and theories on Judas' motive, ranging from the desire for a political coup by the Iscariot band to the desire to have a Messiah who could heal any wounded soldier fighting to overthrow the Roman occupation. These are too complicated and heavy on conjecture. I believe the simplest explanation to be the most probable.

My personal opinion is Judas, having seen the Lord escape the hands of angry mobs numerous times, saw an opportunity to either make more money or, more likely, repay what he had stolen from the Lord's ministry. Either way, money was his motivation. His ruse, as I see it, was to betray the Lord Jesus into the hands of the Pharisees and chief priests for the negotiated price of 30 pieces of silver. Then, just as the Lord was to be taken into the custody of the officers, Jesus would escape yet again, or so Judas anticipated, as He had at other times and in similar scenarios. Judas would be 30 pieces of silver richer, and no one would be the wiser, or so Judas assumed. Alas, his scheme did not go as planned.

Little did Judas know that his flirtation with sin for three years had slowly set him up to be *the* traitor—*the* son of perdition. Little did Judas realize that his sticky fingers in the Lord's purse were slowly opening his heart for demonic possession, and not by some lowly demon but by satan himself (John 13:27). Judas discovered that all sin pays a wage and one never knows when the paycheck clears.

All too late, Judas realized what he had done and proclaimed, "I have sinned in that I have betrayed the innocent blood" (Matt. 27:4). His flirtation with sin cost him more than just his eyesight and his life; it cost him his salvation. By flirting with his sin in his private life, Judas had been slowly hanging himself for over three years. Don't be a Judas and don't be a Samson! Quit flirting with your sin.

Chapter 7

DESTRUCTIVE SECRET No.3-
Ignore Your Weaknesses

One of the beauties of the Bible is that it doesn't shy away from the ugly realities of life or the shortcomings of its historical figures. Both the successes and failures of all of the Bible heroes are on full display. Noah built a famous boat (and the first zoo) but also had a wine problem. Abraham obeyed God, left his hometown and became the father of our faith, but he was also fearful and prone to lying about his relationship with Sarah. Moses was a tremendous leader and the meekest among men, but he had a short fuse—first striking down an Egyptian as a young man and later striking the Lord's rock as an old man. Gideon overcame timidity and fear to become a great judge, only to lead Israel into idolatry near the end of his life.

Eli knew the voice of God and successfully trained Samuel, but he permitted his own sons to become perverted priests. David was a great king, military strategist, and worshiper, but he was also an adulterer and a murderer. Solomon was humble and the wisest of kings, but he married hundreds of heathen women and introduced their pagan idols into the temple of his namesake.

Even the Apostles of the New Testament are shown with all of their shortcomings and flaws; Peter's anti-Gentile prejudice and loud mouth, Judas' betrayal, Thomas' doubt, James' and John's furtive move to obtain the seats at the Lord's left and right hand, even Paul's disobedience to the Holy Spirit concerning a certain trip to Jerusalem.[18]

These were real people with real problems and real weaknesses. Their stories are recorded for our admonition, edification, and education. God's desire to use them in spite of all their flaws should be an encouragement to us, yet there's no reason for us to repeat their failures.

The biblical account of Samson is just as honest, and it presents us with a dire warning. One of the morals of his tale is that neglected weaknesses will always grow up to trump the greatest strengths. We have already covered Samson's two greatest weaknesses: his loner attitude and his unbridled sexual appetites. As we observed, his lack of interaction and accountability to others only allowed his sexual lust to grow unfettered. It would be foolish to believe he was ignorant of these two gaping problems in his life. He knew the Law. He very clearly demonstrated to Delilah his understanding of the Nazirite vow and all of its implications upon his life. Samson was not ignorant. He was reckless.

God Promotes the Flawed

What we see in the life, ministry, and destruction of Samson is a pattern played out over and over again today. God promotes flawed people to positions of leadership everyday because He does not look for perfect people, just perfect (mature) hearts. If the Lord could only use perfect people no one would qualify. The Lord appoints men and women to places of leadership while they are yet works in progress, knowing there are still heart issues to be resolved, sin to be mastered, gaps in sound doctrine, and weaknesses to be fortified. (How merciful of God!)

---

[18] Paul violated numerous warnings from God *not* to go to Jerusalem (Acts 20:21-23; 21:4, 10-12). Acts 19:21 reveals that Paul's forbidden trip to Jerusalem was something he "resolved in his attitude" to do. The closer he got to Jerusalem the more intense the warnings became. Paul refused to be moved by the warnings. Not only did he *not* get to preach the Gospel to the Jews or address the saints at Jerusalem, but he ended up in prison for two years without being able to preach the Gospel until he was called to stand before Festus and King Agrippa (Paul's Two Years of Silence, Acts 24:27).

God promotes based on what He sees in the private lives of His saints. He is looking for humility (1 Pet. 5:6), faithfulness (1 Tim. 1:12), and the desire to change (2 Cor. 3:18). God promotes people He finds trustworthy, though they will always be flawed. This means God will promote you, not because He loves you, but because He trusts you. Understand that just because God loves you doesn't mean He trusts you. And even if He trusts you, it doesn't mean you're perfect.

God promotes us based on the trajectory of our lifestyles. If we demonstrate a pattern of serving God, conquering sin, overcoming weaknesses, and obtaining victories in our lives, then He expects us to maintain that lifestyle trajectory as He adds more responsibilities to our lives. Don't be deceived: God's promotion does not mean your life is flawless, it just means you've done well so far.

If and when God's promotion comes, it is no time to take your ease. Once God has promoted you, your workload for Him actually increases. Not only are you now responsible for the new assignment, but you must also maintain the private walk with Him that advanced you this far. As Philippians 3:16 exhorts, "however, let us keep living by that same standard to which we have attained" (NASB). The worst thing we can do is neglect the lifestyle that earned the promotion as we sit back and enjoy the benefits of the new position (see Luke 12:16-20). The promotions of God cannot be tenured; that is, they are not secured once and for all. If we once qualified, we must *stay* qualified. The higher the Lord promotes us, the more He will require of us. We are not permitted to draw back unto perdition (Heb. 10:39).

Samson was promoted and became a judge even with flaws in his life, but the grace of God covered those flaws . . . for a season. I believe we can safely assume that, as with most young men, the early seeds of sexual temptation were present in his life, as were perhaps his tendencies to isolate himself. These weaknesses were not major or significant enough to disqualify him from ministry in the beginning, but they would require attention and correction if he were to successfully continue in leadership and finish his race.

This brings us to a critical truth in God's Kingdom: we are not permitted to stay the same. God expects us to grow up and advance. The callings of God are always upward. He calls us to higher standards, higher morals, greater successes, greater endeavors, and greater heights in Christ. As we grow in the knowledge and grace of our Savior, His toleration for sin in our lives rapidly shrinks. Growth in Christ means raising the standard, and God expects us to come up higher. He expects us to address our weaknesses.

Boulders, Cobbles, Gravel, and Sand

When we are first born again, God permits boulder-sized issues to exist in our lives. After all, we are just babes in Christ. But as we grow in our walk with Jesus, the Lord raises the standard and shrinks the tolerance to, say, cobble-sized issues and sins. As we continue to grow, the Lord expects even more out of us, and again the standard rises, the tolerance shrinks, and now He only tolerates gravel-sized sin and rebellion. The Lord continues to call us to run our race, laying aside weights and even more sins as He raises the standard again. Yet a little more growth brings us to a sand-sized sin tolerance, then a silt-sized, and finally clay-sized particulates. This process never ends. We will be dealing with sin, rebellion, and flesh until we lay aside our bodies—but that's part of growing and maturing in Christ.

Samson failed this process and chose to ignore his weaknesses. The increasing power of God in his ministry created tighter and tighter standards in his private life—standards he consistently violated. Though his weaknesses started off small, manageable, and even possibly "tolerable" for a season, the holes in his morality only enlarged as his ministry grew. Samson's downturn began the day his anointing surpassed his character. Can your personal character sustain your public anointing?

Neglecting Weaknesses Can Lead to Apostasy

In a passage chronicling the dangers of apostasy, the book of Hebrews presents a startling spiritual concept concerning the relationship between the presence of God and private sin:

> **For the earth which drinketh in the rain that cometh oft upon it, and bringeth forth herbs meet for them by whom it is dressed, receiveth blessing from God: But that which beareth thorns and briers is rejected (reprobate), and is nigh unto cursing; whose end is to be burned. But, beloved, we are persuaded better things of you, and things that accompany salvation, though we thus speak.**   **Hebrews 6:7-9**

This passage uses the allegory of rain and farming to explain the spiritual causality behind apostasy. Here, the earth (or land) receives the rain that waters everything equally. In this parable, the land is neither good nor bad, but the seeds already sown in the ground will determine the land's harvest.[19] The land that receives the rain and produces good things receives blessings from God, while the land that receives the same rain and produces wicked things is rejected and is near to being cursed by God.

The good land is good because it has been carefully tended, and the bad land is bad because it has been neglected. If the bad field is too far overrun with briers and thorns, the farmer will have no choice but to burn the field and start all over, this time paying closer attention. We know this passage speaks to the Christian's relationship with Jesus Christ because the author concludes with the encouragement to the reader that they (the author and his companions) were convinced of a better outcome for the Hebrews than that of a cursed field.

---

[19] In contrast to the parable of the Sower and the Word (Mark 4:3-20) where the ground is the variable and the seed-type remains constant, here the ground is the constant and the seed sown is the variable, e.g. herb seeds compared to thorn and briar seeds.

The heavier implication is that the Holy Spirit's presence, represented here by the rain, moves upon our lives, causing everything that has been sown in our life to spring up—both good and bad alike. This is not to say that the Spirit of God sows bad things in our lives—not at all! But the Spirit of God is life-giving, like the rain, and it causes *everything* to spring up.

I want to be careful not to say that the presence of God causes sin to grow, but Paul addressed this spiritual phenomenon another way by saying, "I had not known lust, except the law had said, Thou shalt not covet," and "but sin, taking occasion by the commandment, wrought in me all manner of concupiscence. For without the law sin was dead," and "but when the commandment came, sin revived, and I died" (Rom. 7:7-9). In a sense, the Law actually "brought to life" sin and death in response to the divinely spoken Word of God.

Perhaps then, we can safely say that the presence of God's Spirit causes *everything* to spring up, if for no other reason than for the gardener to attend to it and weed out the wicked things. That is why this passage of Scripture emphasizes the need for a "dresser" or cultivator of land (lit. *to practice agriculture*). The Holy Spirit causes the cultivated areas of our lives to produce beautiful, praiseworthy fruit for our God while also causing the neglected areas of life to be revealed as sinful and carnal. If we ignore these weaknesses, they will only continue to grow and bring certain pain and demotion. For this reason, we cannot afford to neglect our known weaknesses once the Spirit of God has exposed them.

Everyone Has Weaknesses

We all have weaknesses. Humble people will acknowledge their weaknesses, but wise and prudent people will actually do something about them. It will always be our weaknesses that bring us down. As we covered in Chapter 6, "It's the little foxes that spoil the vine." Our strengths require no attention. In the face of our strengths, it is very tempting to ignore, bury, and even turn a blind eye to our weaknesses, but make no mistake about it—weaknesses must be addressed!

We can't outrun our inadequacies; we must strengthen and fortify them. We can't fix our weaknesses by magnifying our strengths. There's no quick fix for our weaknesses, so we need to stop looking for one. Personal weaknesses must be solved, trained, adjusted, confronted, and disciplined. They must be tended so they don't become the briars in our otherwise beautiful garden for God. If we only live in our strengths, we willfully turn a blind eye to our own demise. We should be like the great revivalist John Wesley, who, having become convinced it was impossible to live as "half a Christian," decided to catalogue his weaknesses and establish rules to overcome them.[20]

When your strengths are as great as Samson's were, it's easy to see how it might be tempting to ignore any personal weakness. After all, someone so anointed is too mighty to fail, right? As previously covered, Samson's shortcomings were his isolationism and his unbridled lust. No doubt, these two worked in tandem to guarantee his ruin. But if he had only shored up his weaknesses, if he had only addressed his flaws, his story would have certainly had a different ending. Samson chose to foolishly ignore his weaknesses and trust only upon his strengths, all to his own downfall.

Oh, the fallacy of magnifying personal strengths while downplaying one's personal weaknesses! If we would stop and consider that our quality of life (be it Christian maturity, mental stability, natural success, family, health, etc.) is brought down by our weaknesses, we would never choose to ignore them. In fact, the quickest way to improve your average in life is to pull up the lowest number—that is, improve your greatest weaknesses first. It seems that the prevailing wisdom in some cultures, even some church cultures, is to magnify one's strengths and act like there are no problems. This is not reality. This is not faith. This is lunacy. Real Christians have real weaknesses, and real weaknesses need real help.

---

[20] Bruce Shelley, *Church History in Plain Language,* (Nashville, TN: Thomas Nelson, 2013), 349.

The Trinity to Help Our Weaknesses

Likewise the <u>Spirit also helpeth our infirmities</u> <u>(weaknesses)</u>: for we know not what we should pray for as we ought: but the Spirit itself maketh intercession for us with groanings which cannot be uttered. And he that searcheth the hearts (Jesus) knoweth what is the mind of the Spirit, because he maketh intercession for the saints according to the will of God (the Father).   Romans 8:26-27

The Apostle Paul, by the Spirit of God, indicated in Romans that we have infirmities—plural, as in more than one weakness. Paul continued his teaching in this passage by emphasizing only one of the many weaknesses we possess as Christians: the weakness of ignorance in prayer. So Paul starts his subject very broad and then instantly narrows his emphasis to one point: prayer. He then points out that we have so many weaknesses that the Holy Spirit must make intercession for us with unutterable groanings, and not just the intercession of the Holy Spirit, but also the working of the entire Trinity on our behalf.

These two verses reveal an interesting process the Trinity is constantly working in our lives regarding our infirmities. The first step of this process begins with the divine plan that our Father has for our lives. This individualized divine plan is the blueprint by which our lives must be built. The second step involves the Lord Jesus searching and judging our hearts (Ps. 139:23-24; Jer. 17:9-10; Rev. 2:23) according to where we are in relation to the Father's divine plan for lives. In essence, Jesus inspects us in comparison to the divine blueprint much like a building inspector would, looking for any construction that might be out of spec. Finally, the Holy Spirit makes intercession for us regarding where we fail to match God's specifications, helping us to make repairs and stay in the center of God's will for our lives, thus ensuring we fulfill our destiny and run our race to the end. Hebrews 12:1 reminds us that there is a race set before us. Not every Christian will finish their race. It is possible to make heaven without finishing your race. I personally believe most Christians won't finish their race simply because most of them never begin to run it.

This divine process has caused me to often wonder just how weak am I that the entire Godhead must constantly intercede on my behalf to keep me in the will of God. It's a sobering question. However, be forewarned: the intercessory work of the Trinity is only *one* of the many ways God helps our weaknesses. We cannot falsely believe that the Holy Spirit is taking care of our weaknesses; therefore, we no longer have any. There is still a large role for us to play in our own betterment. We still have a responsibility when it comes to personal maturation.

A Simple Remedy

As a pastor, I have taught my church a very simple remedy for fixing any personal problem, and though simple and effective, it does take time and consistency. The solution is simple: find five or six Bible verses that address the problem at hand and then pray those verses over your life everyday—multiple times a day if necessary—until the problem is resolved. (This may take years, but it's better than dying a failure.)

For example, if your marriage is your biggest weakness or if it's under attack, I would immediately suggest two passages that must be prayed daily: 1 Corinthians 13:4-8 in the Amplified Bible and Ephesians 5:25-29 (for the husband) or Ephesians 5:22-24 (for the wife). I recommend praying the famous Corinthian love passage something to the effect as follows:

> *Father, I pray in the name of Jesus, that I know I am born again and your love is in me and works in my marriage; therefore, I declare that I can and do endure long and I am patient and kind. I declare that because of Your love in me, I am never envious or jealous, nor am I boastful or vainglorious, displaying myself haughtily. Your love working in my life causes me to*

> ***never be conceited, arrogant, rude or unbecoming . . .***
> ***(1 Corinthians 13:4-5)***

Now a prayer for the husband from Ephesians 5:25-29:

> ***Father, I thank You that I love my wife even as Christ***
> ***loves the Church. I declare I give myself for my wife***
> ***that I might sanctify her and cleanse her, washing her***
> ***with the Word of God. I declare that I love my wife***
> ***even as I love my own body and I nourish and cherish***
> ***her even as the Lord does the church . . .***

I think you get the picture. Prayer is our number one tool to change things in our lives. It by no means undermines any necessary action that must be taken in the natural; rather, it fortifies our natural actions and can even cause them to become more effective. Don't neglect your weaknesses. Pray the Word of God over them and be changed!

The Fivefold Ministry Gifts

God wants His children to mature. We are called to constantly change from glory to glory even as by the Spirit of the Lord (2 Cor. 3:18). This cannot be accomplished by ignoring weaknesses. The very concept of maturation implies that there are successive stages of growth and pruning where weaknesses and inadequacies are confronted, strengthened, and fortified.

The New Testament references four stages of Christian maturity: babes in Christ (1 Cor. 3:1), little children (1 John 2:12-18), young men (1 John 2:12-13,18), and fathers (1 Cor. 4:15). Unfortunately, the most common term the Bible uses to address the saints is "little children." This may prophetically imply that most Christians will never mature beyond that stage of Christian growth.

Some spiritual growth can take place alone in prayer and Bible study, but it is impossible to fully and accurately mature on your own.

Maturation requires help. We must also keep in mind that aging doesn't always mean maturing. The passing of time makes one old; growing in the grace and knowledge of Jesus Christ makes one mature. It is possible to be genuinely born again for 30 years and still be a babe in Christ. For such an individual, 30 years passed by and their bodies have aged, but their soul has remained immature and underdeveloped. God understands the propensity of this phenomenon, so He gave "gifts unto men." Ephesians tells us He gave apostles, prophets, evangelists, pastors, and teachers:

> **For the equipping of the saints for the work of service, to the building up of the body of Christ; until we all attain to the unity of the faith, and of the knowledge of the Son of God, to a mature man, to the measure of the stature which belongs to the fullness of Christ. As a result, we are no longer to be children, tossed here and there by waves and carried about by every wind of doctrine, by the trickery of men, by craftiness in deceitful scheming; but speaking the truth in love, we are to grow up in all aspects into Him who is the head, even Christ.**
>
> **Ephesians 4:12 (NASB)**

It's interesting that the Bible describes people with ministry endowments as "gifts." Like all gifts, these were given to bless us. I'm thankful that Paul not only listed these ministry gifts (also often called *ministry offices*), but he also told us what purpose they serve. The job descriptions of these offices reveal many things to us as believers.

The first job description assigned to the minister is that of "equipper." This informs us that we cannot be properly equipped to serve God without the work of these men and women in our lives. They equip us so we can fulfill our Christian service of good works. For the Body of Christ to be built up, the individual believer must maintain good works.

The second purpose and ability of a ministry gift is their assignment to mature the Body. This also implies that the Body of Christ cannot be fully matured without the fivefold ministers performing their duties.

Paul evinces four facets of maturity in this passage. First, maturity is defined as "unity of the faith." This speaks of our ability to fellowship with one another without squabbles or discord, illustrating a biblical social life centered around the saints, not heathen. Second, maturity requires "knowledge of the Son of God." This describes our need to expand our knowledge of Scripture and build sound doctrine. Third, Paul uses the term "mature man" or "fully-grown man" to convey a larger picture of maturity beyond the spiritual arena of doctrinal maturity and Christian fellowship. Finally, Paul uses another broad phrase indicating an even higher standard: "to the measure of the stature which belongs to the fullness of Christ." The New Living Translation records it as "measuring up to the full and complete standard of Christ." That's a lofty endeavor and one that cannot be accomplished on one's own, or by ignoring one's weaknesses. And yet, Paul, by the Holy Spirit, taught that we, the Body of Christ, have been given ministry gifts—men and women anointed of God—for the purpose of helping us to attain to the "full and complete standard of Christ."

We need these ministers in our lives because we can't always see where we are wrong. We all have spiritual blind spots and can't always see our weaknesses. When we do see our problems, we're not always so motivated to make the changes. That's when the Gospel minister will be called upon by God to confront our lives and provoke us to do better.

> **Herald and preach the Word! Keep your sense of urgency [stand by, be at hand and ready], whether the opportunity seems to be favorable or unfavorable. [Whether it is convenient or inconvenient, whether it is welcome or unwelcome, you as preacher of the Word are to show people in what way their lives are wrong.] And convince them, rebuking and correcting,**

warning and urging and encouraging them, being unflagging and inexhaustible in patience and teaching.
2 Timothy 4:2 (AMP)

The Lord's representatives are authorized by Him to tell us in what way our lives are wrong and to show us the solution. That means they're anointed by God to see our weaknesses and hold us accountable. No one, not even a minister, will ever be able to finish their race as a loner. Sure, you might accomplish some great things and even bear some fruit, but starting your race is no guarantee you will cross the finish line. Samson began a great work but never finished it. Imagine what he could have accomplished had he submitted to a spiritual leader.

Even Preachers Need a Pastor

Who tells the preacher when and where he or she is wrong? Preachers, also called ministry gifts, are anointed to perfect the saints, but preachers are saints too; and therefore, they still need perfecting. Every minister needs the influence of the fivefold ministry gifts in their lives even though they are a gift themselves. There is no way around it: every minister needs a pastor, mentor, discipler, or father-in-the-faith.

Semantics aside, the minister must be accountable, correctable, trainable, pliable, humble, meek, and submitted. So, they must submit *upward* to someone greater than themselves. Sadly, most Western ministers, if they believe in submission at all, usually believe in submitting *downward* to boards, deacons, and committees. I suppose these less-than-biblical forms of church government are better than a wild vagabond-style ministry, but true biblical submission is always upward. You *submit* up, you *subject* laterally, and you *lead* those under you. Boards and committees are great for wisdom and some accountability in natural matters, but they can never replace the anointing and graces with and upon a fivefold ministry gift.

Every minister is required by God to submit to someone greater. If you are reading this as a minister and you lack a pastor (mentor, discipler, father-in-the-faith), why? What is your excuse? Is there no minister in the land greater than you? Is there no one whose feet you can sit at to receive personal correction and help? Are you convinced God has no one you can trust? Going to conferences doesn't cut it. Reading a thousand books by your favorite Christian authors won't cut it. As a minister, your life is flawed and your ministry is filled with blind spots and weaknesses you cannot afford to ignore. You need to find someone to submit up to.

You cannot complete your race alone. You must have help from someone greater than you. That is how God ordained it. Some may argue in pride, "I have the Holy Spirit and the Bible; I don't need to submit to anyone," but the Bible describes its own limitations by calling itself not just a mirror, but a "dark puzzling[21] mirror" (1 Cor. 13:12; James 1:23-24). A mirror can only show you one direction at a time. No matter how you may twist or twirl in front of a mirror, you can only see one dimension at a time. To see your blind spots, you must have a second mirror reflecting the blind side of your reflection. A pastor will hold up that second mirror for you and show you what you can't (or don't) want to see. A good pastor will not leave you or your weakness alone, even when you want to. There is safety in submission.

Biblical Examples of Submitted Leaders

It is obvious Samson lacked oversight. He was a vagabond in every sense of the word: *wandering from place to place, carefree life, disreputable, etc.* Samson's parents appear to be the only people to ever attempt to correct him. As loving parents, they tried to point out a weakness in his life, but he resisted their reasonings to his own hurt. Samson isn't alone. There are many biblical leaders who rejected the help God tried to send them through another leader. The evil king Rehoboam rejected the council of his father Solomon's advisors. Even the good king Uzziah ignored the rebuke of Azariah the high priest. Thankfully, there are

---

[21] Greek: *ainigma*—riddle, puzzle; hence English "enigma"

Bible examples of leaders who were not like Samson, Rehoboam, or Uzziah.

Moses (Exodus 18:1-27)

Moses was highly educated in all the knowledge of the Egyptians for 40 years (Acts 7:22), then cross-trained for 40 more years as a shepherd son-in-law to the high priest of God in Midian. He was the instrument of God's power and the mouthpiece of God's declarations. When Moses lifted the staff of God, powerful miracles happened. Concerning power and influence, there was arguably no one in the known world greater than Moses at that time. He was the executive leader of the nation of Israel and yet, when his father in-law Jethro came to visit him, Moses deferred to him, even bowing before him. Aaron and the elders of Israel also deferred to Jethro and came to him in order to worship and sacrifice to God.

For all of Moses' greatness, ministerial success, and anointing, he still had blind spots. In this case, Moses thought he had to handle all the petty squabbles among the Israelites. Jethro could instantly see the problem in Moses' ministry when Moses couldn't. A simple word of correction, "The thing that thou doest is not good," saved Moses from an early death due to exhaustion and discouragement. Thank God Moses had a father in the faith to whom he submitted himself. It helped his weaknesses, strengthened his ministry, and blessed God's people.

King David (2 Samuel 11:1-12:25)

King David's early years were shaped by submission: first to his father, then to King Saul. This critical season of training taught him how to trust the leadership God placed in his life. In fact, David's submission to his father landed him in the fields where he learned to kill the lion and the bear. His submission to his father positioned him at the battle with the Philistines where he could then kill Goliath as easily as he killed the lion and the bear. His victory over Goliath promoted him into King Saul's favor and court.

King Saul became David's next leader. David faithfully served King Saul as armor bearer, worship leader, and comforter; even risking his own life to help the demonized king. His faithful service and submission to the king positioned him for great promotion. David was learning that submission has its benefits. The consistent promotion he experienced reinforced his trust in the leadership God had placed in his life. This vital lesson saved David's life when his greatest weakness manifested decades later.

As we saw in Chapter 5, David began to backslide when he isolated himself in the comfort of his home as his men went off to war. The resulting adulterous affair and murderous cover-up marked the downturn of his monarchy. We often read the story of David's adulterous scandal and overlook the implication of the necessary time required for all the events to unfold. It's easy to read the narrative and envision all the events—adulterous affair, Uriah called home, Uriah moved to the frontlines for certain death, birth of the love child, Nathan's rebuke, David's repentance, and the death of the child—as all occurring in a short time, but this is not the case. From the time of David's adultery and murderous conspiracy until the time of his rebuke by Nathan the prophet and the death of Bathsheba's child can be no less than a year or two, perhaps longer.[22] David's life had been off track for a long time, and he showed no signs of repenting when Nathan rebuked him.

Nathan came with a severe parable to judge and rebuke David saying, "you have despised God's commandment," "you have despised the Lord," and "you have shown utter contempt for the Lord." It is evident that death was all but certain for the fallen king. But David, upon hearing "you are the man!" and realizing how greatly he failed his God, did not

---

[22] Three words are used for "child" in the biblical narrative: *ben, yeled,* and *na'ar; Yeled* is used 11 times to describe the doomed child. These three words are translated "son, male child, boy, offspring, lad, or youth." These words do not imply an infant or baby. The Hebrew words *owlel and yanaq* are used to indicate "suckling, babe, young child, infant, or little one." The implication here is that Bathsheba's first son may have been as old as four or five years of age when he died. This would indicate that God postponed judgment several years after the initial act of adultery and murder.

argue with the prophet or justify himself, but humbly yielded and quickly said, "I have sinned against the Lord." David had learned to trust the leaders God placed in his life. Even though the sword never departed from his house the last 20 years of his life, he was at least able to hear from a God-sent leader, repent, and live another 20 years. David spent the last half of his monarchy preparing for the construction of Solomon's Temple.

King Jehoash (Joash)
(2 Kings 12:1-20; 2 Chronicles 24:1-22)

The life of King Jehoash of Judah is unique because his testimony swings from one extreme to the other. God promoted him through the instruction of a spiritual father, but he quickly fell after his mentor passed away. Jehoash was the son of the wicked king Ahaziah, grandson of the wicked king Jehoram and great grandson of the good king Jehoshaphat. King Jehoram (Jehoash's grandfather) should have followed in Jehoshaphat's footsteps, but he married Athaliah, the wicked daughter of Ahab and Jezebel. (Note to young men: Don't fall in love with Jezebel's daughter). Queen Athaliah then was the mother of King Ahaziah and the grandmother of King Jehoash. This genealogy is important in order to follow the whole story.

Queen Athaliah was very wicked and cutthroat. When her husband Jehoram became king, he killed all his brothers (the other sons of Jehoshaphat). He forsook the God of his father Jehoshaphat and built idolatrous altars in the high places and caused the people of Jerusalem to commit fornication. Elijah testified against Jehoram and prophesied his destruction. Part of the judgment of God against Jehoram and his wife Athaliah was that wickedness would befall his children and wives. In time, Arabians came to kidnap and murder Jehoram's other wives and all his children except Ahaziah. The hand of God further moved against Jehoram, and he became sick until his bowels fell out and he died.

His only remaining son Ahaziah then became king at age 42. He was just as wicked as his father and Jehu killed him after only a one-year reign. When the wicked widowed Queen Athaliah saw this, she flew into a rage and moved to kill all the royal descendants that could be king (these would have all been her children, grandchildren, or step-children). One child escaped her rage—Jehoash. The deceased king Ahaziah had a sister named Jehosheba who had married the priest Jehoiada. This sister rescued Jehoash, her nephew, when he was only one year old, hiding the baby and his wet nurse in the Temple. Jehoida and his wife Jehosheba raised the child in secret for six years while the wicked Athaliah played queen and mocked God.

Finally, after six years, Jehoida the priest determined it was time to coronate the boy-king and overthrow the wicked Athaliah. He enlisted the help of the priests, and with much pomp and ceremony, anointed Jehoash king of Judah at the tender age of seven. When Queen Athaliah heard of the priestly coup, she ironically declared, "Treason, Treason!" Jehoida had her drug out of the Temple and killed before the king's palace. Thus, Jehoash's 40-year reign began with the execution of his wicked grandmother.

Jehoash, only seven years old when he was appointed king over Judah, was blessed to have Jehoiada the priest as an adoptive father, spiritual father, mentor, and instructor. Jehoash obtained a biblical reputation only ascribed to six kings, "he did that which was right in the sight of the Lord."[23]

The instruction of the priest Jehoiada sparked a zeal in the young king's heart for the house of God. He observed how it had suffered much damage and idolatrous corruption at the hands of the sons of Athaliah, so he gave a commandment for the priests to begin repairing the Temple. By Jehoash's twenty-third year as king, the priests had still failed to complete the repairs. This irritated the king. At this exact season, Jehoash's mentor and adoptive father, Jehoiada the priest, was now high priest and directly responsible for the priests' negligence. This called for a unique situation where the mentor was corrected by his more zealous

---

[23] The other five kings were Amaziah, Uzziah, Jotham, Hezekiah, and Josiah.

mentee, much like Samuel as a child prophesied against his mentor Eli (see 1 Sam. 3:11-21).

Jehoash famously called for the chest with a hole bored in the lid to be placed at the entrance of the Temple in order to collect the tax Moses had commanded for the Tabernacle's maintenance (Ex. 30:12-16). The damage to the Temple must have been significant because the amount of money collected is described as "money in abundance," which was spent on masons, builders, carpenters, metalworkers, and supplies. After much work, the temple breaches were repaired and strengthened. King Jehoash left as his legacy this honorable Temple repair project, a legacy that would have been impossible without the influence and instruction of a spiritual father in his life.

Eventually, Jehoiada died at age 130, leaving Jehoash without a godly leader. Soon after, the idolatrous princes of Judah began to pull the king's ear and steer his heart. It can easily be argued that after decades of discipleship, Jehoash should have been solidified in his faith and convictions, but the heart is deceitfully wicked and can be stolen given enough time and subtle speech (cf. 2 Sam. 15:1-6). Jehoash's weakness was that he could easily be steered. This is good if you have righteous influences around you, but it can be lethal if you fall into wicked company.

With wicked counsel in his ear, King Jehoash soon abandoned the Temple he worked so hard to rebuild, and he led Judah into worshipping Asherah poles and idols. Unsurprisingly, this provoked the anger of God. As is often the case, the Lord's wrath first manifested as rebuking messages from several prophets sent to call Judah and Jehoash to repentance. With the voice and influence of one ministry gift—the priest—gone from Jehoash's life, the Lord was trying to expose the king's weakness through the voice of another ministry gift—the prophet. Since Jehoash's weakness was that he seemed to eagerly listen and follow the advice of whoever had his ear, perhaps the voice of a righteous prophet might turn his heart back to Jehovah. Sadly, the king turned a deaf ear to every prophet the Lord sent to testify against him.

In what can be described as a final act of mercy, the Spirit of God anointed one of Jehoiada's biological sons, Zechariah. Surely the corrupted king would honor the Word of the Lord coming from the mouth of his beloved mentor's son—his own adoptive brother. Zechariah prophesied against all of Judah:

> **Thus saith God, Why transgress ye the commandments of the LORD, that ye cannot prosper? because ye have forsaken the LORD, he hath also forsaken you.   2 Chronicles 24:20b**

Jehoash responded by having the people stone his adoptive brother in the courtyard of the Temple. As he lay dying, Zechariah looked at Jehoash and said, "May the Lord see this and call you to account."

Because of the king's unrepentant heart, the Lord continued to dial up the judgment. After the murder of Zechariah, the Lord sent a small company of the Syrian army to Jerusalem. They overthrew a great host of Israelite soldiers and killed all the princes of Judah (presumably the ones who bent Jehoash's ear), plundering their substance. The attack left Jehoash wounded and sick, and the Syrian army only retreated after he bribed them with great treasures and gold from the same temple he worked so hard to restore. And still, for all these rounds of divine judgment, Jehoash never repented or called out to God. Two of his servants killed him while he lay in bed recovering from his injuries.

What a sad ending for a king who had done such great things for God Almighty. There was absolutely no reason for him to fail. He was adopted and raised in the Temple by the premiere priest of his day, who continued to instruct him even as king. Jehoash's downfall came when he listened to the wrong voice. Though the Bible doesn't record how long Jehoida lived and influenced Jehoash's life, Jewish history claims that Jehoida died in the thirty-eighth year of Jehoash's 40-year reign. That means Jehoash outlived his mentor by only two years before his servants murdered him. Imagine laboring well for 38 years and then blowing it the last two years. Jehoash listened to the wrong voices, and it cost him his life and ministry.

If only he would have allowed others to point out his weaknesses. Jehoash, who once rebuked the entire priesthood for neglecting God's House, died an unrepentant idol-worshipping traitor who abandoned the same Temple he once fervently contended for. He listened to the wrong voices and rejected the counsel of God's leaders. Don't start strong only to come up short like Jehoash. Don't cut short your ministry like Jehoash.

What are your weaknesses? What are the things life is requiring you to master, but you haven't yet? What are the excuses you offer in defense of your weaknesses? Excuses do nothing but *excuse* you from the promotions of God. Quit making excuses! We are much better off than Samson. Not only are we born again when he couldn't be, but we have been given three tools to master our weaknesses: the Trinity's intercession, personal prayer and Bible study, and the leadership of the ministry gifts. There's no reason for any Christian to ever fail like Samson. Please know, you'll never advance beyond your weaknesses, so don't neglect them.

Chapter 8

DESTRUCTIVE SECRET No. 4-
Allow Your Strengths to Deceive You

In His divine wisdom, God has blessed every person—believer and non-believer alike—with a set of strengths and weaknesses. We excel at some things and yet absolutely struggle at others. Once we are born again, God endows every believer with new supernatural graces—abilities that weren't in us before the New Birth. Romans 12:6-8 lists these grace gifts as: prophecy, service, teaching, exhortation, giving, leadership, and mercy. (Grace gifts are often referred to as *The Seven Grace Gifts of the Father*, cf. *The Nine Gifts of the Holy Spirit* in 1 Corinthians 12:8-10, and *The Five Ministry Gifts of the Son* in Ephesians 4:11. How wonderful that the entire Trinity wants to help the Church through a total of 21 gifts!)

The Romans Chapter 12 grace gifts are divine abilities God places in each one of us, and they differ from the 1 Corinthians Chapter 12 gifts of the Spirit. Christians can activate the grace gifts as they please, whereas the gifts of the Spirit only manifest as God wills (1 Cor. 12:11). The Romans 12 grace gifts are also different from the Ephesians Chapter 5 gifts of the Son, which are the fivefold ministry callings only given to some Christians. In total, there are 21 gifts given by the Divine Trinity to help the Church glorify the Lord Jesus Christ! Sadly, some Christians and denominations believe that 12 of these 21 gifts have passed away; therefore, their churches and lives only operate at less than half capacity.

Concerning these Romans 12 grace gifts, 1 Peter 4:10 exhorts the believer to "be a good steward" of their graces and to use them one toward another. Simply put, these graces are supernatural strengths and abilities—they don't require work to cultivate or develop. Some practice may be necessary to fine tune them, but these are what we would call personal strengths. In the local church it might be said of one member, "Boy, they sure are great with kids," and of another, "Goodness! They have a natural presence in the pulpit," and of yet another, "They are always such an encouragement," or finally, "He's a natural leader isn't he?" These statements recognize the various graces or abilities God placed in His servants (specifically the grace gifts of service, teaching, exhortation, and leadership, respectively).

However, these giftings or abilities can be deceptive. How so? Just because God graces you with a great teaching ability doesn't mean you're a great husband. Or just because you're anointed to sing and lead God's people in praise and worship doesn't mean you have your appetites under control. Having a grace to sing doesn't mean you manifest the fruit of self-control. And just because you're graced in the business realm and generous in your financial giving, doesn't mean you're an acceptable student of the Bible.

In short, just because God has gifted you doesn't automatically mean He is currently pleased with you. My first pastor often preached the strong warning God once spoke to him: *Just because I'm using you doesn't mean I'm pleased with you.* Or to put it another way: don't allow your calling to deceive you.

Being used of God can often be misleading. Not that God is misleading anyone, but there can easily arise a false sense of security when the hand of God is upon us. I want to make it very clear: when God uses a person, He does so to bless His people. We should never become prideful when the gift of God upon our life is in operation.

God does not bestow His abilities upon mankind for mankind to get the credit. The gifts are given to bless mankind so that God would receive the glory. Don't be high-minded. God will use someone despite them for His people's sake (just think of Balaam or Judas). God will honor the grace He placed upon your life even if you aren't honoring Him with your private life. At first glance, this concept may seem counterintuitive, confusing, or even contradictory, but I believe the danger here will become evident as we proceed.

When God calls a man or woman to a place of leadership within His Kingdom, He places a special endowment of grace, anointing, and ability upon them. The supernatural promise of God's help via His abiding presence is the only thing that ensures a leader's success.

God appeared to Abraham and made this same promise to him—the promise of His presence and help. God did the same with Isaac and Jacob. He rekindled these promises with Moses at the burning bush and again with Joshua at the passing of Moses. The promise of God's abiding presence and supernatural ability followed the same pattern each time: "I will be with you, My presence will be with you, and you will succeed at the task I have assigned you."

Every minister ever called by God knows exactly what I'm talking about. Every preacher used by God consciously or unconsciously understands the implications of this unique covenant: "I only succeed because God is with me. If He doesn't help me, I can not accomplish His assignment." This unique ministry covenant is called many different things in the body of Christ. Many refer to it as "the calling." Some call it "the anointing." Sometimes it's referred to as "the gifting" or "the grace." Regardless, they are all speaking about the same thing—God's hand upon His chosen vessel to accomplish the unique assignment given to them. This calling was present in the life of Samson, allowing God to use him – despite his private perversions.

Samson had two special graces: the first grace was to be a leader and the second grace was to begin to break off the Philistine oppression from Israel. We have previously seen that he never walked in his first grace— that of tribal leader. His second grace, however, is the one that has propelled him to infamy for millennia—the grace to deliver Israel from the Philistines, by whatever means necessary. Samson's gifting was an anointing that guaranteed no Philistine could ever get the upper hand or win against him. From the account provided of Samson's life, one thing is clear: as long as Samson was consecrated to God, no Philistine could stand in his way.

Samson Learned His Limitations

Samson began to be moved and stirred by God's calling on his life while in his youth. We already established that he had no mentor or discipler to aid him in his development, so it is safe to assume he was self-taught in his special gifting. His confidence is evident in the relaxed demeanor with which he carried out the exploits against the enemies of his people. Samson never showed any fear in the face of the Philistines as Moses did at the thought of returning to Egypt or as Gideon did toward his father and the Midianites.

Samson casually slew 30 Philistines in order to obtain 30 changes of clothes. He flippantly burned a city's entire harvest without fear of the ramifications. He carelessly tore gates off a city while the enemy was crouching at the same gates. He never feared instigating a fight with a Philistine family, a Philistine city, or a Philistine army. In fact, Samson grew to be very comfortable coming and going from the midst of the Philistines and their cities, even living the last season of his life among them. This is the confidence of a man who knows his gifting and its limitations.

Samson's ministry was on a meteoric rise. As he began to test the limits of his calling, his exploits became more and more daring; killing first a lion, then 30 men, then the "hip and thigh" slaughter at Timnath, then 1,000 men at Lehi. But here is the contradiction of his life: as Samson's public ministry grew more and more powerful, his private life grew increasingly perverse. Just because God was using him publicly didn't mean God was pleased with him privately.

As we previously noted in Chapter 2, Israel's judges were limited in their domain and assigned enemy, that is, they weren't called of God to pick fights with every enemy nation in every direction. Samson was no different. He wisely learned to "stay in his lane," noting the limitations of his gifting. He never pursued conflict with the Midianites, the

Amalekites, or even any remaining Canaanites. Why? Because he knew he wasn't anointed to fight those enemies. He stayed right in the midst of the Philistines (cf. Josiah's unauthorized war against Pharaoh-Necho, 2 Chronicles 35:20-24). His life's activities are recorded as having only taken place in eight cities, many of them less than 10 miles apart, right in the thick of Philistine country. In fact, his entire life was lived in an area approximately 20 miles by 40 miles square, or 800 square miles[24] (see Map 4).

Samson also understood that his supernatural strength didn't work against fellow Israelites. When the men from Judah came to Samson to deliver him over to the Philistines, he adamantly requested that his brethren swear an oath not to slay him themselves (Judges 15:12). Samson's request heavily implies that the men of Judah could have easily killed him even when scores of Philistines couldn't. Why? Because Samson was only anointed to kill Philistines, not Israelites. Unlike many modern preachers, he understood the limitations of his calling.

Samson submitted to his fellow Israelites and the bondage of their new ropes without any fight and walked down to the awaiting Philistine army. It was as he approached the Philistine camp, but only *after* the Philistines began to cheer *against* him, that the Spirit of the Lord came upon him to slay them. Why? Because Samson was only anointed to slay Philistines. He knew this and wisely stayed in his ordained grace, and so he continued to succeed.

The Miracles and Deception of Samson

The uniqueness of Samson's ministry is ascribed to his supernatural strength and the miracles that followed his life. The exact number of events that can be counted as miracles is debated among theologians, but I put the number at 10. I have omitted the miracle spring at Lehi (Judges

---

[24] For perspective, this means Samson's domain was approximately the combined area of two U.S. cities: Nashville, TN (526 mi^2) and Chicago, IL (234 mi^2).

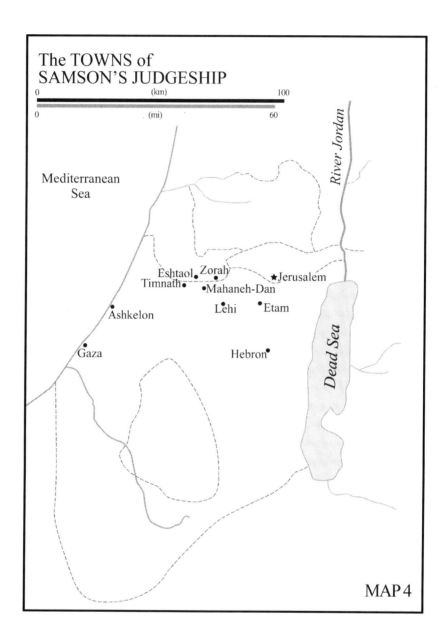

The TOWNS of
SAMSON'S JUDGESHIP

MAP 4

15:19) because I count that as something God did *for* Samson, as opposed to the other 10 miracles that I classify as something God did *through* Samson. Here are the 10 miracles God did *through* Samson:

1. Slaying the lion barehanded (14:6).
2. Slaying 30 men in Ashkelon (14:19).
3. "Hip and thigh" slaughter of the Timnites (15:7-8).
4. The breaking of the two new cords as if they were burnt flax (15:14).
5. The slaying of 1,000 Philistines with a donkey jawbone (15:15).
6. The removal of the gates of Gaza (16:3).
7. The breaking of seven green cords like yarn when it touches a flame (16:9).
8. The breaking of new ropes like a thread (16:12).
9. The breaking of the weaver's loom (16:14).
10. The destruction of Dagon's temple (16:30).

Patterns of Deception

In this list of miracles arise two patterns. First of all, the miracles reveal a notable increase of power and anointing. The first thing Samson killed was a lion, followed by 30 men, then the "hip and thigh" slaughter, then 1,000 Philistines, and finally, more Philistines in his death than in his life (more than 3,000). One could not mathematically plot a more exponential increase in power. Had he not short-circuited his life, there is really no telling how many Philistines he would have eventually put down—maybe all of them.

The second pattern is the relationship between the increase in the miracles and the increase in Samson's sinful private life. As discussed in Chapter 6, when Samson should have been growing cleaner, holier, and more influential, his private life was, in fact, becoming increasingly sinful. There is an uncanny relationship between the escalation in his feats of strength and his sexual perversion. This pattern manifests through the events surrounding his interaction with the three women in his life.

With the Timnite marriage, his feat of strength killed 30 men from Ashkelon to appease a wedding party commitment. When his father-in-law gave his wife away (the marriage having never been consummated), Samson responded by burning up the local crops of the village of Timnath. This exploit affected more people than did slaughtering 30 men in Ashkelon for their clothing. When the Timnites reacted by killing Samson's wife and father-in-law, he exacted his revenge with the "hip-and-thigh" massacre. Even on this occasion, there is a very visible escalation of power and retribution. It should be noted that this series of events occurred during the beginning of Samson's ministry, when he appears to be clean from sin and controversy.

The herculean judge's most bizarre feat of strength involves the second woman in Samson's life, who was a harlot. This event should have never taken place, but his encounter with the Gazite prostitute placed him in a dangerous situation, required divine deliverance to escape, and resulted in a confusing miracle. It may be hard to fathom, but Samson performed one of his greatest miracles after he paid to have sex with a prostitute.

The Bible records that Samson tore the Gaza city gates from their hinges and carried them away "bar and all." This miracle was only possible because it occurred at a Philistine city while Philistines threatened Samson's life. This feat would not have been possible at a Hittite city or an Amorite city, at least not by Samson.

This victory is very deceptive because, right before Samson was anointed to tear the city gates from their posts, he was effectively not anointed at all as he fornicated with a Philistine prostitute. How confusing and misleading for one of God's chosen leaders to be in the throes of sinful passion one minute and in the next moment anointed mightily to not only escape a Philistine ambush, but to totally demoralize an entire city by literally tearing its defenses from its hinges. Had the Gazites proceeded with their intended ambush on Samson, there would have most certainly been an even greater slaughter than the 1,000 at Lehi. As it was, the Gazites stood down and no Philistine blood was shed that day.

I fully believe this manifestation of divine strength, despite nearly simultaneous sexual sin, was the final act of self-deception for Samson. This is the last miracle Samson performed against a Philistine before his suicide in the Temple of Dagon.

Samson allowed his God-given strengths to deceive him into a false sense of security and invincibility. He lost sight that it was the Spirit of God upon him doing the miracles, not he himself. Oddly enough, when he was clean he could only tear a lion in half, but when he was dirty, he could tear the gates off a city. It can definitely be said of Samson that just because God used him publicly doesn't mean God was ever really pleased with him in private.

The Final Woman

Enter Delilah, the final woman in Samson's life. She was a Philistine woman with whom he permitted his heart to fall in love, and still the anointing on his life continued to abound. Even in Delilah's bedchamber, the increasing robustness of Samson's bonds was matched by the ease with which he escaped.

He was first bound with seven bowstrings only to break through them like yarn when it touches a flame. Then he was bound with new ropes, which he broke as if they were a mere thread. And finally, Delilah wove his seven massive locks of hair into a giant room-sized weaver's loom. Unbeknownst to him, when he sat up from his sleep, he tore apart the loom and walked out with the weaver's beam still in his hair. From these supernatural escapes, we can observe how the more perverse the sin, the stronger the anointing grew in order to deliver him.

We see a New Testament reflection of this spiritual principle in Romans 5:20, "For where sin abounds, grace does much more abound." The greater the sin, the greater the grace required to escape it. If we compare sin to a deep pit into which one has fallen, then what one requires is rope to escape. If the pit is 20 feet deep, 20 feet of rope will be insufficient for rescue. There must be extra rope to anchor off to a tree, boulder, or vehicle. In essence, if sin abounds 20 feet, the rescuing rope of grace will need to "much more abound"—say, 30 or 40 feet.

But even in the New Testament there is a limit to grace. Should we sin to get more rope? God forbid. There was a limit to which the power of God could increase on a perverted Samson, and there is a limit to the grace of God today; otherwise we could easily change the grace of God into lasciviousness.

God's power continued to increase in hope of delivering Samson, but each deliverance only resulted in him going even deeper into sin the next time. Samson eventually crossed the line and God left him. I compare it to a light bulb blowing out because it cannot handle the power flowing through its filament. Be sure your private character can handle your public anointing.

Samson's Final Miracle

The once great warrior, the terror of Philistia, the gallivanting Nazirite beholden to none was now a blind, bald slave to his mortal enemies. His glorious strength was gone. The blind warrior was chained to a grinding wheel, then between two pillars in a pagan temple, made to dance and entertain pagans, led around by the hand by a young boy. But it was in that sad and pitiful condition the anointing came upon him the mightiest. After grinding corn as a mere mortal for a few weeks, Samson's hair began to grow back.

Here we see the reinstitution of the Nazirite vow. He was, in essence, starting his vow all over again. With his renewed consecration came the renewed power to destroy Philistines. Chained between two support columns, he prayed the second and final prayer ever recorded in his ministry: a request for death. Like Moses before him and Elijah after him, Samson requested to die. But unlike these men, Samson's death request was motivated by shame and vengeance.

In his final act as a judge of Israel and representative of the one true God, he pushed apart the pillars supporting the temple of Dagon and killed more Philistines in his death than in his life. It was an act of suicide for he was now utterly hopeless, an act of vengeance for his two eyes' sake (Judges 16:28), and an act of anointed judgment against the wicked Philistines. According to Jewish tradition, because of the catastrophic suicide of Samson and subsequent temple destruction, the

Philistines remained subdued for 20 years in order to make sure he had no sons who might have inherited his strength.

Samson Replaced

I have learned in ministry that everyone is replaceable. I find it rather humbling that Jesus declared that rocks, much less fellow human beings, could replace us. Samson was no different. According to Kantor,[25] Eli the priest began to judge Israel the last year of Samson's life. Samson was being replaced even before he died. Also, the day Eli became high priest, Hannah entered the tabernacle seeking God for a child—Samuel. Samuel would grow up to replace Eli after he died a failed judge and priest.

Everyone is replaceable. God will move until He finds someone who will obey Him. He *will* have His will accomplished. Though Samson began to deliver Israel out of the hands of the Philistines (Judges 13:5), it was Samuel who actually completed the job (1 Sam. 7:13). God will always find a replacement. Your private perversion is training your replacement, and one day you might meet them.

A Deceived Worship Leader

Let us now look at the pattern of Samson in the context of modern ministry. Consider the gifted worship leader who has a massive fight with their spouse on the way to church. Though they may not have resolved the marital rift before service begins, he or she will still be used of God to lead His people into His presence because that is what He has anointed that worship leader to do. Is the worship leader right with God? Not if he or she hasn't been reconciled to their spouse. Yet God will still use them once the music begins.

You can clearly see how being used of God in this situation has the potential to hurt the worship leader's life. If they perceive a tremendous anointing in that song service and if they see how God used them to help

---

[25] Mattis Kantor, *The Jewish Time Line Encyclopedia*, 41.

His people, they could falsely assume God is backing them over their spouse in their marital argument. If our hypothetical worship leader isn't careful, he or she might begin to think God's divine use of them during a worship service is His endorsement of every other area of their life. Nothing could be further from the truth. Their strength—the worship gift—could end up being the greatest source of deception in their life. Just because God has used them in their grace publicly does not mean He is happy with them in their private life.

A Deceived Preacher

Consider someone with another divine grace gift—the preacher. Gospel preachers have special giftings and anointings from God to preach, expound, and teach God's Word. The shyest of preachers changes into a different person once they stand before people with the task of setting forth God's Word. This is their grace. This is what they are created to do. It doesn't matter what kind of day they have had. It doesn't even matter how they feel in their body. The moment they approach the pulpit to teach God's people or approach the stranger to evangelize them, the gift of God upon their lives will be activated and God will use them mightily.

Does this mean their private life pleases God? Not necessarily. Does this mean God endorses everything in their private life? Not at all. This simply means they are a vessel that yielded to the gift of God upon their life at the moment their gifting was needed. When that moment of divine use passes, all secret sins still await them back home. All marital tensions still require attention. All unrestrained appetites still demand prayer and restraint. If the preacher isn't careful, he or she might begin to think God's divine use of them to preach, teach, or win souls is also His endorsement of their entire life. Just because God uses them in public does not mean He is happy with them in private.

King David was a prime example of this spiritual principle. David had many strengths divinely granted him by God. He was a fearless warrior and brilliant military strategist. He was a man after God's own heart and one of the greatest worship leaders in the Bible. He was by far the most prolific psalmist and an inventor of many musical instruments. David honored God with all his heart and ability, and God gave him great success everywhere he turned. But these strengths overshadowed his hidden weaknesses.

King David may have foolishly asked, "With so many strengths, how can I possibly fail?" He sadly discovered halfway through his reign that it wasn't his public strengths that brought about his shame and fall. It was his private weaknesses. His strengths, in a sense, deceived him.

Thriving Under the Need

When my wife and I were first set in as the pastors of our church, I quickly experienced what countless preachers before me already knew: when you answer God's call, He will be there to help!

The first year we pastored, my wife and I both worked fulltime jobs. We were also newlyweds. There were a lot of brand new variables in our lives during that initial season of pastoring, and yet I found that pastoring and administrating the church came quite easily. Helping the sheep was easy. Learning to steer our church was easy. Making executive decisions was easy. Preaching and teaching three services a week was easy. I initially worried that I wouldn't succeed at pastoring, but God's presence was ever tangible and so was His help.

Please don't misunderstand me. Everything was work and many long days were (and still are) required, but the success the church was experiencing was nothing less than supernatural. This was the gifting and calling on my life doing what it was designed to do—to help me, the vessel of God, accomplish the will of God for our church.

Everything was going better than I had expected at the church until my wife made a profound and painful observation, which furthered my investigation into this subject of Samson and ministerial self-deception.

After several months of marriage and pastoring, my wife came to me more than a little hurt and said, "The more these people (the church family) need you, the more you thrive. You're always ready to jump to their need."

"Yes," I declared. "I do thrive. It's what I'm anointed to do—I pastor these people."

"Sure," she replied, "but don't forget that I need you too, and you don't seem so eager to jump to my aid."

What can you say to that but "I'm sorry"? With my wife's subtle rebuke, I began to take note of how much easier it really was for me to pastor God's people than it was for me to husband[26] my wife. Why? Because the anointing to pastor a church does not transfer over to marriage. There is no ministry anointing to be a husband. The pastoral anointing doesn't carry over to my relationship with my wife. To put it another way, my wife needs her husband to be a husband, not a pastor, and there is no special super-pastoral-husband anointing. There is a grace to pastor and there is a grace to be a husband, but pastors don't get a special husband grace that other men don't get. No, we get the same one as every other man, and it still requires a lot of work.

Men tend to track where they are wanted and where they are successful. As a younger pastor, I was excelling and succeeding much more quickly at pastoring than I was as a new husband, so I began to give myself more to the ministry than to my marriage. I found pastoring to be a lot easier than being a newlywed, and why? Because there was no special anointing to be a husband. A few hours of prayer and labor produced much greater results in the church than it did for my marriage. I had yet to learn that I must husband my wife just like any other Christian man—through prayer, trial, error, repentance, and practiced selflessness. Sadly, I was on track to be a much better pastor than I was a husband. I was allowing my ministry successes to deceive me.

Understandably, many ministers fall into this dangerous trap. They find that ministering can be easier (I didn't say easy, just easier) than marriage. If the minister is a pastor, his constant interaction with God's people can satisfy any social interaction needs he may have, leaving him exhausted and socially sated when he returns home. This in turn can

---

[26] I have intentionally used "husband" as a verb throughout.

make his wife feel second-class. Jealousy can easily be aroused in the heart of a minister's wife and understandably so. Many a preacher has been rightly accused of having an affair with the Church.

The ambition in many preachers will drive them to save the world at the cost of their families. Ministers must learn to keep all things in their proper order: always God first, always spouse second, third children, and ministry last. Should you get any of these out of order, your marriage and family won't be an epistle worth reading, and that would certainly disqualify you from ministry (see 1 Timothy 3:1-13).

Like Samson standing before hostile Philistines, many pastors have learned that they come alive when God's people need them. It's what they're made to do. Regrettably, these men risk becoming better ministers than they are husbands and fathers. This can ultimately result in children who become the stereotypical rebellious and god-mocking "preacher's kid." It can also result in divorce or extra-marital affairs. Such horrific ministry failures only serve to confuse God's people and bring a blot to the holy name of Jesus Christ. The landscape of modern Church history is replete with the names of once famous preachers fallen to the trash heap of shame and failure. Mastering your private life is hard work, but you shouldn't gain the world and lose your family. Just because you're a good preacher, teacher, pastor, or evangelist doesn't automatically mean you're a good father, parent, friend, or wife.

Female Ministers

Female ministers must be cautious to keep their calling in line with God's Word. God has clearly demonstrated that He has and will continue to use women in ministry roles. This is evidenced through the lives of Miriam, the first prophetess; Deborah, a prophetess and the only female judge (she arose "a mother in Israel"); Huldah, an invaluable prophetess in the time of King Josiah's revivals; Isaiah's wife, a prophetess and mother of Mahershalalhashbaz; Anna, the prophetess at the dedication of the Christ-child; the Samaritan woman at the well sent by Jesus to evangelize her people; Mary Magdalene, a "sent one" to "tell his disciples and Peter the he (Jesus) goeth before you into Galilee;" Priscilla, the wife to Aquila, together they were a powerful husband and wife preaching team and helpers to the Apostle Paul; and Phoebe, the deaconess to the entire church of Cenchrea.

The fact that God wants to use women in ministry roles is clear from the previous examples, but the question that must be answered is what impact does a ministry calling have on the non-ministry areas of that woman's life? Specifically, assuming she is married, does a woman's ministry calling trump the New Testament commandment for her to submit to her own husband (Eph. 5:22; Col. 3:18), especially if her husband is not a minister? There seems to be much confusion on this subject in our post-modern, post-feminist society, but the answer is quite easy to deduce from the Scriptures.

Before God instituted ministers and ministries, God instituted marriage—one man in covenant with one woman until death do them part. The Bible is clear (though offensive to modernists) on the role between husband and wife—the woman was made for the man:

> **Neither was the man created for the woman, but the woman for the man. Nevertheless neither is the man without the woman, neither the woman without the man, in the Lord.**   **1 Corinthians 11:9,11**

Following the hermeneutical principle known as the Law of First Mention,[27] the creation of marriage preceded the creation of ministry; therefore, marriage takes precedence. This is confirmed simply in 1 Corinthians 11:3, "the head of a woman is her husband" (RSV).

Scripture does not authorize a woman's ministry calling to hijack her marriage and lead her home. There is absolutely no biblical precedence

---

[27] The 'Law of First Mention' is the principle in the interpretation of Scripture which states that the first mention or occurrence of a subject in Scripture establishes an unchangeable pattern, with that subject remaining unchanged in the mind of God throughout Scripture.

for this. The five ministry giftings of Jesus (Eph. 4:11-12) are for the perfecting of the saints for the work of the ministry. The ministry gifts are not for steering the home or guiding the marriage. Therefore, her calling is to help the Body of Christ as a ministry gift, not to steer her household as a pastor or prophetess over her husband.

Outside of the pulpit, she is simply a Christian woman, wife, and mother. She is no more authorized to steer her household than any other fellow sister in Christ. At home, the married Christian mother will have to fall into her God-ordained role like every other person in the Kingdom. Just like Samson wasn't constantly anointed to slay Philistines, the female minister isn't always anointed to lead the Body of Christ. She's not anointed to perfect the saints when she's at home.

Other misunderstandings on this subject arise from a lack of sound doctrine concerning submission, authority, and domains of authority. Samson only had authority in Dan and Judah and only over the Philistines. He had no authority in Benjamin, Issachar, or Zebulon, and he was not anointed to slay Ammonites or Canaanites.

As a pastor, I have authority over my local church, not the church down the street. I am called and authorized to perfect the saints, but this calling is only effective outside of my church on the occasions when I have been invited into another church or Bible school to do what I am authorized to do. When I get home to my family, I am no longer a pastor but a husband and father. Even as a husband I don't get to use my ministry calling over my wife. Furthermore, my ministry authority isn't valued, respected, or activated much outside of the church world. Why? Because it is for "the perfecting of the saints." It's not for the perfecting of the school district, the local Rotary Club, or the soccer team.

It is beyond the scope of this book, but Christians really need to learn the nuances of submission, authority, and the proper applications of authority. The ministry wife doesn't stand in her ministry office when she gets home anymore than I stand in my pastoral office at the local gym or grocery store checkout line. The authority of my pastoral office doesn't trump the checkout lady's authority to scan my groceries and require my payment. The checkout lady could even be a church member whose wedding I officiated and whose babies I dedicated, but when I am in her domain, under her authority, I must submit to her. She is, after all, under the authority of her employer and accountable to them. She may be glad to see me, her pastor, come through her checkout line, but in the end, she will tell me what to do and I will obey.

Likewise, my pastoral authority doesn't trump the police officer's authority when I am in his domain, nor does it trump the judge's authority if I am present in his or her courtroom. In the same manner, a woman's ministerial authority will never trump her husband's head-of-household authority when she's at home in his spiritual domain. To believe otherwise is gross biblical error.

As a final example, let us consider the domain of a local church. As a younger pastor, many of the guest ministers I invite to come and minister at our church have been in fulltime ministry almost as long as I have been alive. Many are pastors of their own churches. They are tremendous leaders in the Body of Christ and possess decades of experience and wisdom (this is why I invite them). By far, they outrank me in the Lord's Army, yet I've never had a single guest minister try to steer my church or usurp my authority over our local flock. Not once!

These tremendous servants of God (men and women) come, minister the Word of the Lord, teach, preach, exhort, lay hands on the people, sing, and do anything and everything that can be done to perfect God's people, but never have any of them ever tried to steer my church. They stood in our church's pulpit with the authority I delegated to them, using the time allotment permitted, and they manifested their giftings, callings, and anointings to do what God sent them there to do.

When they are done ministering, the service is always turned back over to me, the local pastor. Then, there is always an opportunity, a moment, for me as the bishop or principal of the flock to either approve of what has just taken place or, if need be, correct what may have been preached or demonstrated. Why? Because though these great men and women might outrank me in the Kingdom, they will never outrank me in the church that the Lord has set me over. I will give an account for my local flock, the guest minister will not. In the same manner, the female minister married to a non-preacher must realize that she might outrank her husband in terms of the Kingdom ministry, but she will never outrank him in their home or marriage. This would be a violation of God's divine order.

To the lady minister, the ministry takes work, but there is a divine power to aid you. Your private life will take even more work and there is an anointing to help you; it just isn't your ministry anointing. You must master your private life like every other Christian. If any minister, male or female, undermines or harms their marriage for the sake of ministry, they will be deemed unfit for ministry. God will never promote a Jezebel—no matter how great a prophetess she may fancy herself (see Rev. 2:18-29). Don't let your ministry calling destroy your marriage.

Preachers of Compromise

We have seen the terrifying pattern that the anointing of God will often increase the more a preacher compromises—but only to a point. This becomes the deception of the anointing. Not that the anointing deceives—certainly not! But the minister who knows in their heart that they have compromised God's Word and His ethics, and yet they see the crowds grow larger, the salvations increase, the offerings increase, maybe even the miracles increase—they can begin to falsely believe they are right with God and He is endorsing them. Let us be clear: This is not God endorsing their dirty lifestyle! This is not God endorsing the perverted preacher! This is God using a vessel He chose to anoint for the sake of His people. This is grace abounding much more where sin abounds. But this grace has a limit just as it did with Samson, and there will come a time when the Lord's grace and help will depart from that minister, causing their life and ministry to implode just as Samson's did.

I have seen this scenario play out numerous times in my lifetime. Modern church history is full of famous ministers whose crowds, incomes, and testimonies seemed to swell exponentially right up until they were exposed as embezzlers, sexual perverts, adulterers, or worse. What was going on? Did they pioneer those sins in their lives overnight? Certainly not! They began to slowly compromise their walks with God, here a little, there a little. These famous ministers were often embezzlers for years before they were exposed. They were serial adulterers for years before they were caught. They were womanizers for years before they were ever discovered. And yet the anointing of God would still manifest upon them each time they took the pulpit or went on the air. Why? Because God will always manifest through His chosen vessel to answer the cry of faith. Like Samson, God was using them even when their private lives were filthy and vile—but only to a point.

Perhaps the most terrifying verse in the Bible for ministers is found in the life of Samson. It is the verse that pinpointed the beginning of the end for our legendary Danite: "And he awoke out of his sleep, and said, I will go out as at other times before, and shake myself. And he wist (knew) not that the LORD was departed from him" (Judges 16:20). How utterly terrifying for a minister of God to awake from a slumber, perhaps after a season of backsliding or spiritual apathy, and try to rekindle their walk with God only to find that it's too little too late.

How terrifying for a minister to decide in their backslidden state (and yes, it's very possible for preachers to backslide while preaching in the pulpit two and three services a week) to return to their fervency for Christ only to discover that whatever red line should never have been crossed, was in fact crossed, and crossed without even realizing it. Samson knew not that the Lord had left him. The anointing was gone. The tide turned in favor of his adversaries, never to return to him in the same fashion again. His ministry was over. In that moment, he was a slave and didn't even know it, and yet the worst was still to come.

But how does this happen? Christians in general, and ministers in particular, become overly dependent upon their anointing. Rather than practicing what they're preaching, they ignore their private weaknesses and rest on their public graces. They rely solely on their gifting, never praying or studying the Bible on their own. They build their lives upon their ministry callings and not upon their Christian character, which requires a walk with God. I hate to pull back the curtain on modern Christian ministry, but many ministers today have little to no private walk with Jesus Christ. Many no longer pray in private, study the Bible in private, or live clean in private. They merely play minister on service days, trusting that God will, once again, anoint them in front of the people. How dangerously presumptuous they are!

Samson proved that without a relationship with God you can play minister, but only for a season before the whole house comes crashing down on you. His troubled ministry proves a minister can know how to be used by God without really knowing God. The Bible records only two prayers in the entire ministry of Samson, and both were when he was in dire straits (Judges 15:18; 16:28). Samson never had a relationship with his God, and honestly, neither do many preachers and Christians. They falsely assume their anointing is God's endorsement of their private lifestyles. They learn how to operate in their gifting and calling. They learn the limits and abilities of the anointing on their life, and they wisely stay in that arena.

Like Samson, they learn that if they're anointed to kill Philistines, it's not wise to provoke an Amalekite. They're not anointed to fight Amalekites, so they stay away from them, and the Midianites, and the Gittites, and the Amorites, etc. They learn the boundaries of their gifting and they stay there. This is all well and good and advisable, but the problem is that being anointed in front of Philistines on behalf of God's people is not the same as being anointed at home.

Having a special anointing to kill any and every Philistine is not the same as having a special anointing to beat lust or anger or gluttony or addiction or depression or any other personal problem. Like Samson, New Testament ministers have a special anointing to beat the national enemies of sin (and help the Church), but they don't have a special anointing for their private lives. There is no special anointing to defeat secret sin.

Ministers must beat their private enemies just like everyone else—through prayer, faith, consecration, sanctification, humility, discipline, and getting help. Samson perfectly reflected the spirit of his age—"And every man did what was right in his own eyes" (Judges 17:6; 21:25). Unfortunately, many preachers today also reflect the same spirit of our age—they're doing what's right in their own eyes. I pray you are not someone who publically manifests the Spirit of God, but privately personifies the spirit of the world!

Chapter 9
FINAL THOUGHTS-
A Proverb Versus an Epistle

The legacy of Samson has never been embraced as a pattern for success. He has never been held as a role model. No one seems to want to name their son Samson, their dog maybe, but not their child. Parents name their children after the Bible "greats": Abraham, Isaac, Jacob, Sarah, Rebekah, Rachel, Leah, Ruth, even Gideon or Moses. There's even a famous Elon (Musk). But no one seems to go for Samson. His name is associated with perversion and catastrophic failure. Samson's legacy has succumbed to the biblical curse of becoming "a proverb and a byword."

> **And thou shalt become an astonishment, a proverb, and a byword, among all nations whither the LORD shall lead thee.** **Deuteronomy 28:37**

> **Then will I cut off Israel out of the land which I have given them; and this house, which I have hallowed for my name, will I cast out of my sight; and Israel shall be a proverb and byword among all people:**
> **1 Kings 9:7**

> **And I will set my face against that man, and will make him a sign and a proverb, and I will cut him off from the midst of my people; and ye shall know that I am the LORD.** **Ezekiel 14:8**

In the Old Testament, God again and again judged the unrepentant. One of the numerous judgments God would bring upon a person was to turn their name and legacy into a proverb and byword.[28] The Israelites, like most people, wanted to leave honorable legacies and noble namesakes. Many scriptures bear witness to this fact (see Ps. 9:5-6; 112:6; Prov. 10:7; 22:1; Eccl. 7:1). The promise of God to perpetually mire their name or their family's name was a strong motivator. After all, who wants to be known as disreputable?

The term "proverb" refers to a sentence containing a point of ethical wisdom, often juxtaposing the positive and the negative. Proverbs can succinctly show what *not* to do or who *not* to be like. They offer an object lesson of sorts. In context, the biblical threat of becoming a proverb infers a negative connotation. No Hebrew would ever want to be immortalized in a negative proverb, and neither should we. Due to his sexual sinfulness, Samson could have easily been the inspiration for Proverbs 2:16-22 or 5:3-14.

A "byword" is translated as a *sharp word, a taunt, an insult* or as Dutton's Basic Bible[29] calls it, "a name of shame." This word is used in the Old Testament to describe the harsh, cutting remarks Israel's enemies would make against her when she failed her God. Combined, these two words meant to warn Israel that betraying God would result in them becoming the object of scorn and ridicule to all surrounding nations. This concept is illustrated in the Gospels when Jesus taught the parable of the tower builder:

For which of you, intending to build a tower, sitteth not down first, and counteth the cost, whether he have sufficient to finish it? Lest haply, after he hath laid the foundation, and is not able to finish it, all that behold it

---

[28] See also 2 Chronicles 7:20; Job 17:6; 30:9; Psalm 44:14; 69:11; Jeremiah 24:9.

[29] *The Basic Bible containing the Old and New Testaments in Basic English*, (E.P. Dutton and Co., Inc., 1950).

**begin to mock him, Saying, This man began to build, and
was not able to finish.   Luke 14:28-30**

The failed tower builder became a parable and a byword. Everyone mocked and jeered at him and his endeavor. I'm sure the abandoned foundation stood as a village landmark for a failed endeavor. Like the tower builder in the parable, Samson began with noble intentions but failed to finish what he started, giving the Philistines opportunity to mock him in the temple of their pagan god.

The heart of the tower building parable is this: weigh the cost of following Jesus and be sure you're committed to the very end, lest the world mock you for failing. Too many Christians follow in Samson's footsteps and become a proverb and a byword. They begin a great work for God but fail to stay faithful unto the end.

In the region I pastor, Christians have successfully earned the byword "tightwad." The local restaurant servers dread working on Sundays because the after-church crowd is notoriously cheap when it comes to tipping. Servers sarcastically joke, "Well of course they can't leave us a tip, they just gave all their money to God." So entrenched is the byword of "cheap" in my region that I teach my church to be generous tippers in an endeavor to counter the "stingy Christian" reputation.

Heathen America stereotypes all Christians as hypocrites. "Hypocrite" has become our byword. It is our taunt, our insult, and our name of shame. It's not a fair byword because not all Christians are hypocrites, but it's still the reputation of the American Church.

Countless modern ministry scandals, mostly involving television ministries, helped produce another byword—"televangelist." Televangelist has nearly become synonymous with huckster, swindler, fraud, fake, phony, etc. (I say this as a pastor with a small regional television ministry.) A great majority of disgraced television ministers had genuine Gospel callings upon their lives and a desire to reach people for Jesus Christ, but they failed to master personal weaknesses and temptations. Greed, lust, or pride (or a combination of all three) brought them all down, giving way to the televangelist archetype. Blah!

Many years ago, when the Lord began to deal with me about going on television, I reminded Him of the televangelist's proverb and byword. I told the Lord, "I don't want to be on television. I don't want to be lumped together with all the corrupt preachers bilking your people for money. I don't want people to think I'm anything like them." The fall of television "Samsons" has made it difficult for holy, righteous preachers to use that tremendous tool for the glory of God. Suffice it to say, God ignored my preferences and we began producing a weekly telecast.

Carnal Christians and failed ministers following in the footsteps of Samson develop these pejoratives and stereotypes—tightwad, hypocrite, huckster, and televangelist. Please know, dear Christian, when you fail as Samson did, you can make it very difficult for the rest of us who remain faithful to Jesus Christ. Let me remind you of a very strong Bible warning:

> **For if after they have escaped the pollutions of the world through the knowledge of the Lord and Saviour Jesus Christ, they are entangled therein, and overcome, the latter end is worse with them than the beginning. For it had been better for them not to have known the way of righteousness, than, after they have known it, to turn from the holy commandment delivered unto them.   2 Peter 2:20-21**

Human Epistles

In contrast to being a proverb or a byword, the New Testament teaches us we should aim to be an epistle—a living letter—a lifestyle that can be read of all men.

> **Ye are our epistle written in our hearts, known and read of all men:** **2 Corinthians 3:2**

The NIV continues:

> **You show that you are a letter from Christ, the result of our ministry, written not with ink, but with the Spirit of the living God, not on tablets of stone but on tablets of human hearts.** **2 Corinthians 3:3 NIV**

God wants every Christian to aspire to be an epistle that anyone and everyone can read, not a byword or proverb to avoid. Some people will never read the Bible or attend church, but if your life is an epistle—a letter from Christ—they can still be reached with the Gospel. In reality, the concept of being a human epistle, ready to be read by anyone, is just another way of saying, "be salt and light."

Your life will either lead someone to glorify Jesus Christ and inspire others to be like Him, or your life will be a proverb to avoid, an example of how *not* to be. Epistle or byword—it's your choice. Strive to be an epistle that can be read and followed by all men. And by all means, DON'T BE A SAMSON!

Acknowledgements

Special thanks to Eva and Kiley for the countless revisions, editing sessions, and last minute mark-ups. I am grateful for Darrell's graphic design expertise and keen eye in arranging the cover layout. I also wish to thank Bobbie, Emma, and Pastor Chace for their proofing, feedback, and doctrinal critiques. I am grateful to have a pastor and mentor in Dr. Mark T. Barclay. No doubt, many of his thoughts, teachings, and expressions have made their way into this book. Thank you to Engrafted Word Church for all their support and obedience to the Gospel of Jesus Christ. I'm honored to pastor such a tremendous body of believers. And special thanks to my wife, Manda—not just for the maps that she produced for this book, but for being my greatest support and my very best friend.